Day-VII Archi
A Catalogue of

MW00807785

;

Day-VII Architecture
A Catalogue of Polish Churches post 1945

Izabela Cichońska / Karolina Popera / Kuba Snopek
Photos by Igor Snopek and Maciej Lulko

DOM
publishers

Contents

INTRODUCTION

This photograph taken accidentally by Max Avdeev in 2013 launched our interest
in Polish post-war churches

Day-VII Architecture: Absorbing Modernities

In 1914, it made sense to talk about a "Chinese" architecture, a "Swiss" architecture, an "Indian" architecture. One hundred years later [...] architectures that were once specific and local have become interchangeable and global. National identity has seemingly been sacrificed to modernity. [...]

Ideally, we would want the represented countries to engage [with] a single theme – Absorbing Modernity: 1914-2014 – and to show, each in their own way, the process of the erasure of national characteristics in favour of the almost universal adoption of a single modern language in a single repertoire of typologies.

– Rem Koolhaas, Statement by the Main Curator of the 2014 Venice Biennale

Over 3,000 churches were built in Poland between 1945 and 1989, despite the socialist state's hostility towards religion. We call this Day-VII Architecture. Built by parishioners using materials that were scavenged or pinched, the churches were at once an expression of faith and a form of anti-government protest. Neither legal nor prohibited, the building of churches in this period engaged the most talented architects and craftspeople, who in turn enabled parish communities to build their own houses of worship. Day-VII Architecture emerged against the backdrop of a unique combination of political and social circumstances and is the most distinctive Polish contribution to the architectural heritage of the twentieth century.

The Day-VII Architecture research project began as an exhibition proposal for the Polish pavilion at the 2014 Venice Biennale of Architecture. Rem Koolhaas, the Biennale's chief curator, described the twentieth century as the period when differences between buildings from different cultures melt away; as a time of the complete standardization of vastly distant cityscapes. However, by titling his exhibition 'Absorbing Modernity' he signalled that the reverse of this unification was the appropriation and transformation of global trends by local conditions. The intention behind the Koolhaas Biennial was thus to locate and highlight examples of architecture that, despite raging globalization, reflected something of local culture: architecture with unique local cultural values, original practices of using space or pre-modern methods of construction.

Finding a Polish example that fitted this narrative was not easy. Twentieth-century Polish architects were by no means idle. From scratch they designed not only institutions for a modern state and infrastructure for a modern industry but also millions of flats, twice rebuilding cities that had been destroyed in the two world wars. These efforts, while crucial for our country, nonetheless reflected global developments typical of the era.

But when it comes to the thousands of churches built from 1945 to 1989, an entirely different situation emerged. Arising at the intersection of two mutually exclusive value systems – a secular socialist state and a deeply devout, Catholic society – the form of each of church was always a result of both devotion and protest, aspiration and fear, intransigence and collaboration, tradition and precursorship. Each of these churches is unique, an impossible figure that combines distinct visions of society into a single, paradoxically coherent entity. Drawing on a number of interpretations of modernity from both East and West that intersected on the territory of Poland, the architects of the churches created, together with parishioners, new and absolutely unique architecture.

The first kind of modernity to influence the construction of churches was anti-religious Soviet communism. When, in the wake of World War II, Poland found itself in the Soviet sphere of influence, a struggle against organized religion began on Polish soil. Over the next four decades, this process displayed many and varied faces. During Stalinism, the repressive state apparatus was wielded to fight religion with force. Following Stalin's death, a period called The Thaw ensued, in which the Church and the government attempted to communicate and even to cooperate. The legacy of this short experiment can be seen in the exceptional, albeit never realized, projects that were selected for competitions at the time. When this attempt broke down, a period of rivalry followed that lasted until the fall of socialism. Symbolically, this period began with parallel celebrations of the millennium of the Baptism of Poland (Church), on the one hand, and the millennium of Polish statehood (government), on the other. In retrospect, this rivalry can also be seen as having had an architectural and spatial dimension: the government built schools (as part of the 'One Thousand Schools for One Thousand Years' programme), while the Church erected parish churches.

However, the influence of socialist modernity on churches was not one-dimensional. Throughout the entire period of the Polska Rzeczpospolita Ludowa (the Polish People's Republic, or PRL), the socialist government's intention was undoubtedly to contain the construction of Catholic churches. Paradoxically, however, the PRL's greatest achievements were enablers of Day-VII Architecture and allowed it to reach its ultimate, spectacular form. For, not only did the PRL's centrally planned urbanization transform millions of agricultural labourers into first-generation proletarians, but the industrialization of construction allowed for the creation of large-scale architectural objects. Further, the professional design offices appointed by the communist government educated an entire generation of architects and engineers, teaching them how to collaborate across various levels of hierarchies and professional specializations. Lastly, it was socialism's flagship achievements – such as the eight-hour work day and the free Saturdays won by Solidarity – that provided labourers with enough free time to work on the church construction sites in their parishes.

In the 1960s, the Catholic Church's interpretation of modernity unexpectedly intersected with the socialist approach. Between 1962 and 1965, at the height of the space race, the Church convened the Second Vatican Council, a wide-ranging attempt to reform its structures in the face of rising popular culture, mass society and consumerism. The aim of the Council was to stem the loss of churchgoers and the method it chose was to reform the liturgy. The key term used in the Council documents was 'community'. The Tridentine Mass – a mystical spectacle conducted in Latin with a priest standing with his back to the faithful – was replaced by a mass resembling a meeting of the faithful. Conducted in a local and therefore comprehensible language by a priest facing his people, it aimed to unite and strengthen ties in the local community.

In a way, the Council revolutionized church architecture by chance. The bishops gave no indications as to how the art of building churches was to change; they focused solely on liturgical reform. And yet, the liturgy – the essence of what happens inside the church – is inseparable from its architecture. Every modification, every change in the rite of mass or position of the priest, sparks a chain reaction of fundamental spatial transformations. The post-conciliar mass obliged changes to be made to the spatial design of churches, to their lighting design and to the interior details. The spatial revolution that the architects carried out was thus a by-product of the Second Vatican Council.

In Poland, the implementation of these conciliar changes went hand in hand with a great deal of improvisation. The new rules being introduced at the peak of Cold War, the flow of information to the other side of the Iron Curtain, information concerning both liturgical changes and their interpretation in church architecture, was often delayed and fragmentary. Moreover, Polish architects, unlike their colleagues in the West, were simply not equipped to design churches. Socialist schools of architecture did not teach church design and there was a lack of relevant literature. Eastern European editions of Ernst Neufert's Architects' Data were even shorn of its chapters on sacred architecture. As a result, architects in Poland often had to look to unorthodox sources of inspiration, such as theatre design.

The biggest wave of church construction was triggered by a political event, namely the general walkouts organized by Solidarity in August 1980. Solidarity – a workers' movement calling for reforms to the socialist system – found strong support in the Catholic Church and among the intelligentsia. In the aftermath of the Solidarity strikes, the government, among other things, made concessions to the Catholic Church. In order to alleviate the revolutionary mood, the communist authorities began to issue previously unavailable building permits to build churches. These concessions were, however, merely apparent. Nominally agreeing to the construction, the state did everything in its power to sabotage these projects. It allocated plots of land ill-suited to building; construction equipment, fully controlled by the state, was not made available; and there was no access to building materials, all of which were owned by state companies.

This turn of events meant that churches had to be constructed by parishioners themselves. Local communities sought out architects (sometimes even via organized competitions), acquired building materials and machinery, and managed the construction work, separately and in parallel to existing state structures. The most important postulate of the Second Vatican Council – community building – took root not only in the religious buildings and their designs, but in the very social, grassroots and DIY mode of their creation.

Thus, in the 1980s two disparate modes of architecture developed in Poland in parallel to one another: state architecture and religious architecture. The socialist state produced rational, modernist architecture over the six-day working week (until Solidarity had it reduced to five), while modern industry and infrastructure produced prefabricated housing estates and their accompanying schools, kindergartens and hospitals. This was complemented by Day-VII Architecture, that is the thousands of churches erected among the vast network of housing estates to provide them with a spiritual element, as well as tradition and local identity. Sacred architecture was also a way of articulating protest against the reality of the declining socialist system, a contestation of the political status quo. Last but not least, for the most part it was created by a young generation of architects who were just entering the labour market and who saw designing churches as a way to realize their creative ambitions. This kind of architecture thus needed an entirely new language of expression and postmodernism, which was infiltrating from the West, met this need perfectly.

While the modernist architecture of the first half of the twentieth century was co-shaped by designers from both socialist and capitalist countries, the Iron Curtain disturbed this order. For several decades after WWII, architecture developed separately in the East and in the West, intersecting only occasionally. This is the period during which a new trend that polemicized with modernism – the theory and formal language of postmodernism – emerged in the West. Architects from socialist countries were fully aware of the existence of this new, dynamic and multi-layered architecture: among them book-length manifestos, photographs and postcards circulated. The church construction boom the perfect pretext on which to import postmodern ideas into Poland and thus to bring Polish architecture closer to its western counterpart.

Postmodern forms were perfectly suited to the struggle against the unified socialist landscape. Found in books brought from the West, the elements of this new formal language were adapted to fit the local reality. In the process, however, they took on completely new meanings. Interestingly, the ideas of postmodernists were a perfect match for the challenges faced by designers of Polish churches. Here, for example, the postmodern call to return to tradition fell on fertile ground: the Church wanted to be seen as the guardian of national heritage and as a link with Polish history. After decades of concrete, prefabricated modernism, there was a return to brick, stone and traditional building methods with the construction of churches. Given the lack of access to machinery, industry or modern-day materials, this move was both ideological and pragmatic.

The same can be said about another postmodern architectural notion: the building-symbol. For church architecture, this symbol is the cross, an inseparable element of every church, whose significance in the PRL was strengthened by the church-state competition for the government of souls. Architects did everything they could to creatively address the question of the visibility and form of the cross. In contrast to the cross, which stands as an integral part of every church, the TV antenna towering over Robert Venturi's Guild House, one of postmodernism's most important icons, appears an exterior element added by force. Even elements of postmodern irony and polemical play with traditional forms came to be implemented in the churches. Slanted, or even levitating, columns turned out to be a perfect solution to the post-conciliar call to create a single space interior with excellent visibility.

The 1980s was the highpoint of this Polish religious architecture. It was Solidarity that made it possible to build churches again, and this longstanding hope met with the creative ambitions of the new generation of architects. Permitted to operate outside of the usual industrial restrictions, these architects welcomed the influx of fresh formal ideas from the West. Moreover, the upsurge in social energies willing to contribute to the construction work was greeted with support from the upper echelons of the church dealing with modern architecture. Paradoxically, however, all these dimensions would be weakened by the collapse of socialism at the turn of the decade. After the fall of the common unifying enemy – that 'godless' political system, communism – the fuel required for collaborative action motivated by protest came to an end. The fact of replacing socialism with a market economy was equally important. The state construction industry either went bankrupt or was privatized; church construction was quickly professionalized, and the grassroots,

DIY method was replaced by one around monetary transactions. Hitherto disparate architectures merged into one.

The construction projects from the Solidarity era continued for around two decades, straddling either side of the transformation from socialism to capitalism in equal measure. Their end more or less coincided with the symbolic unification of Poland and the West, which is to say Poland's accession to the European Union. For this reason, we take this particular era of church construction to be an historic period, one that has now come to an end, and Day-VII Architecture to be a unique legacy of the era of transformation between two systems which not only shaped Poland but the entire world over the course of the twentieth century.

Considered as a complex socio-political and spatial phenomenon, Day-VII Architecture tells us a great deal about the times during which it emerged – both from a local and from a global perspective. Locally, it highlights processes that took place during the years of transformation: the empowerment of local communities, the democratization of Polish society, the remarkable rise of the role of Catholic Church in public life. From a global perspective, though, it remains a paradoxical, rich amalgamation of different views on what modernity might be.

Timeline

Year:	Number of churches under construction:
1945	59

The horrors of World War II come to an end. Dresden is destroyed by Allied bombing raids. Hiroshima and Nagasaki are razed to the ground by atomic bombs launched by the US air force. Nazi Germany and Imperial Japan capitulate shortly afterwards. As a result of the Yalta and Potsdam conferences, Poland finds itself in the Soviet sphere of influence.

1946	78

The trial of Nazi war criminals begins in Nuremberg. According to the first post-war census, Poland's population is 23,929,757, almost 11 million fewer than in 1939.

1947	97

Communist leader Bolesław Bierut is elected President of Poland. The arresting of Catholic priests begins. By mid-1947, sixty priests have been imprisoned. A decision is issued on the location and construction of a model Stalinist city, Nowa Huta, near Kraków. The government of the Polska Rzeczpospolita Ludowa (the Polish People's Republic, PRL) rejects the US Marshall Plan for aid for the region. The Soviet blockade of West Berlin begins.

1948	125

Polska Zjednoczona Partia Robotnicza (The Polish United Workers' Party, PZPR) is formed. The abolition of schools run by the Catholic Church begins. A high land tax on church property is introduced and Polish bishops are banned from travelling to Rome. Bishop Stefan Wyszyński is elected Primate of Poland. The United Nations' Universal Declaration of Human Rights is signed in Paris.

1949   139

The Communist Democratic Republic of Germany and the capitalist Federal Republic of Germany are established. Stowarzyszenie Architektów Rzeczpospolitej
Polskiej (The Association of Polish Architects, SARP) adopts the resolution made
by Party architects on socialist realism. The Church 'delegalizes' communism: a
decree issued by the Holy Office threatens Catholics with excommunication for
belonging to or cooperating with the Communist Party.

1950   149

The Korean War breaks out. The Polish People's Republic begins to implement its
first six-year plan. The Polish Catholic Church refuses to sign the Stockholm appeal
against the nuclear arms race. The first day of May is declared a state holiday. The
Office for Religious Affairs is established. Construction gets underway on Ludwig
Mies van der Rohe's ephemeral Farnsworth House.

1951   140

Władysław Gomułka, leader of the reform-oriented section of the Polish United
Workers' Party, is arrested. The imprisonment of Bishop Czesław Kaczmarek
marks a new stage in the anti-Church activities of the state security apparatus
and the judiciary.

1952   129

Le Corbusier's most famous building based on his residential housing design prin-
ciple, the Unité d'habitation, is completed in Marseille. In New York, the UN Sec-
retariat building is erected. The Polish state intensifies its efforts to end all religion
classes in schools. Thirty-seven priests are arrested. Forty-six higher theological
seminaries are dissolved following an administrative order. The state turns all
requisitioned school buildings into hospitals, workers' hotels or nursing homes.

1953   113

Joseph Stalin dies. The city of Katowice changes its name to Stalinogród (lit., 'Stalin
Town'). In East Berlin, a workers' uprising breaks out and is bloodily suppressed.
The Soviet Union carries out the first successful test explosion of a hydrogen bomb.

1954   **109**

Félix Candela designs the Church of Our Lady of the Miraculous Medal in Mexico, while construction begins on Le Corbusier's chapel at Notre Dame du Haut in Ronchamp. Nikita Khrushchev steers Soviet construction efforts towards total industrialization, full typification and prefabrication.

1955   **106**

A socialist defence pact – the Warsaw Pact – is agreed. Religion classes are still held in thirty-six per cent of Polish schools, but only twenty-five per cent of students attend. A Stalinist skyscraper, The Palace of Culture and Science, opens in Warsaw. Pruitt-Igoe, a housing estate in Saint Louis designed by Minoru Yamasaki, opens.

1956   **112**

During the 20th Congress of the Communist Party of the Soviet Union, Nikita Khrushchev condemns the Stalinist 'cult of personality'. An anti-Soviet uprising breaks out in Hungary and is bloodily suppressed. In Poland, the reformer Władysław Gomułka is elected First Secretary of the Central Committee of the Polish United Workers' Party. An emerging thaw in East-West relations is also reflected in church-state relations. Nearly one million worshippers take part in a ceremony at Jasna Góra Monastery. In schools, religion classes are reinstituted. Construction begins on Lucio Costa and Oscar Niemeyer's design for Brasilia. Le Corbusier's High Court building in Chandigarh, India, is completed. The National Architects' Council in Poland announces the end of socialist realism in architecture.

1957   **148**

Earth's first artificial satellite, the Sputnik, is launched by the Soviets. The European Economic Community is established. In Poland, many permits are issued for the construction of new churches and chapels and the redevelopment of existing ones. The thaw lasts less than a year. A new policy concerning church-state relations is devised: religion is to be confined to churches.

1958   **181**

John XXIII is elected Pope. In Poland, a new directive opposes the issuing of new construction permits for churches. The Social Fund for the Construction of Schools for the Millennium launches the 'One Thousand Schools for One Thousand Years' programme to celebrate the first millennium of the Polish state. By 1972, 2791 schools have been built.

1959

Restrictive tax rules targeting the clergy come into force in Poland. Frank Lloyd Wright's Guggenheim Museum in New York is completed, Oscar Niemeyer conceives the Presidential Palace in Brasilia and construction on Alvar Aalto's Church of the Three Crosses in Imatra, Lapland, is completed.

1960 175

Riots break out due to a ban on the development of a new church in Nowa Huta. Protests turn into clashes that last several hours and cover a large part of the city. Construction is completed on Le Corbusier's La Tourette monastery in Éveux, France.

1961 149

Soviet cosmonaut Yuri Gagarin becomes the first man to orbit the Earth. Construction begins on the Berlin Wall. St. John's Abbey Church in Collegeville, Minnesota, designed by Marcus Breuer, is completed.

1962 127

The Second Vatican Council begins. The US opts to blockade Cuba in reaction to the deployment of Soviet nuclear missiles on the island. One of Warsaw's most important churches, the Carmelite church, is shifted back twenty-one metres due to road construction works. Basil Spence's reconstruction of Coventry Cathedral is completed.

1963 111

Celebrations are held for the 600th anniversary of the oldest Polish higher education institution, Kraków's Jagiellonian University. The Przyjaźń (friendship) oil pipeline from the USSR to the German Democratic Republic (GDR) is launched. Skopje is destroyed by a major earthquake.

1964 104

Nikita Khrushchev is ousted as First Secretary of the Central Committee of the Communist Party of the Soviet Union. SARP meets in Gdańsk to discuss issues of typification in housing construction.

1965   95

In Rome, the Second Vatican Council comes to an end. Polish hierarchs send letters to episcopal conferences in various countries, informing them of the 1000th anniversary of the Baptism of Poland. One of the letters is called Pastoral Letter of the Polish Bishops to their German Brothers, which is well-known for stating, 'We forgive and ask for forgiveness'. The authorities of the Polish People's Republic deem that the episcopate exceeded its authority by referring to foreign policy in the letter. Millennial school number 1000 is built in Warsaw. Kenzō Tange designs the reconstruction of Skopje, and Robert Venturi creates Vanna Venturi House in Chestnut Hill, Pennsylvania, now an icon of postmodernism.

1966   91

In April, celebrations get underway for the Year of the Baptism of Poland in Gniezno Cathedral. Several days later, final celebrations begin for the Millennium of the Polish State, which the political authorities of the Polish People's Republic organize with vigour. Over the next few months, Poland observes two competing celebrations of this event: a Catholic Church-organized celebration of Polish Catholicism and a state-organized commemoration of Polish statehood.

1967   84

The Israeli-Arab Six-Day War begins. Poland breaks diplomatic relations with Israel as a result. Preparations get underway for talks between the Polish People's Republic and the Vatican. Expo '67 begins in Montreal and Buckminster Fuller designs the American pavilion. Frederick Gibberd's Liverpool Metropolitan Cathedral is completed. On the 50th anniversary of the October Revolution, an exhibition is opened in Warsaw called 50 Years of Soviet Architecture.

1968   88

Protests sweep through Europe and the USA. In France, students take to the streets and begin occupying university buildings. After an anti-Semitic campaign, several thousand people of Jewish descent leave Poland. Martin Luther King Jr., pastor and activist in the US civil rights movement, is assassinated. Alexander Dubček becomes the First Secretary of the Communist Party of the Czechoslovak Socialist Republic and the Prague Spring erupts, but is quashed by the armed intervention of Warsaw Pact troops.

1969   **92**

American-crewed Apollo 11 mission lands on the moon. Buzz Aldrin and Neil
Armstrong take steps on the lunar surface. In Poland, celebrations are held for the
25th anniversary of the Polish People's Republic (PRL).

1970   **101**

Chancellor of the Federal Republic of Germany (West Germany) Willy Brandt and
the PRL Prime Minister Józef Cyrankiewicz sign a Polish-German treaty recog-
nizing Poland's western borders. Food price rises result in protests in Gdynia and
Gdańsk. The government brings in the military in December 1970 and forty-one
people are killed. Edward Gierek becomes the First Secretary of the Central Committee of the Polish United Workers' Party.

1971   **104**

Just as the first factory to produce industrialized, prefabricated elements for housing
in Warsaw is being built, a number of buildings on Pruitt-Igoe estate are demol-
ished. In the West, the latter's partial destruction is perceived as the symbolic end
of modernism. A thaw in church-state relations results in the former receiving
ownership of more than four thousand churches and chapels, nearly one and a half
thousand buildings and several hundred hectares of arable land.

1972   **115**

US President Richard Nixon and leader of the USSR Leonid Brezhnev conclude
the SALT 1 disarmament treaty. Robert Venturi's book, Learning from Las Vegas,
is published. Together with Madelon Vriesendorp and Elija and Zoe Zenghelis,
Rem Koolhaas submits Exodus, or the Voluntary Prisoners of Architecture, as his
thesis project for the Architectural Association.

1973   **128**

The Sydney Opera House, designed by Jørn Utzon, is completed. A law is passed to
enable the Polish state to transfer more than six hundred properties to the Catholic
Church. Oscar Niemeyer and Kenzō Tange visit Poland.

1974   **145**

During his stay in Rome, the Minister of Foreign Affairs of the Polish People's
Republic, Stanisław Olszowski, invites the head Vatican diplomat, Archbishop

Agostin Casaroli, to make an official visit to Poland. The Archbishop stays in Warsaw from 4 to 6 February 1974 and is received with the full honours reserved for the diplomatic head of a sovereign state.

1975   **174**

Communal flat number 1,000,000 is built in Warsaw.

1976   **186**

Economic crisis grips Poland, leading to sugar rations. Increased food prices trigger social protests. The opposition Committee for the Defence of Workers is established. The Polish Bishops' Conference asks the highest state authorities not to suppress workers taking part in protests against increased food prices.

1977   **214**

On 1 December, Edward Gierek and Pope Paul VI hold a meeting. Adam Michnik's book, Kościół, lewica, dialog (The Church and the Left) is published, in which the author attempts to establish a platform for dialogue between the left-liberal formation and Catholicism around a common struggle to defend human rights.

1978   **243**

Polish Cardinal Karol Wojtyła is appointed Pope. He chooses the name John Paul II. In Poland, 144 factories are in operation to produce prefab elements for the housing construction industry. Kraków's urban architectural complex and the salt mine in Wieliczka are included on the UNESCO world heritage list. Rem Koolhaas publishes Delirious New York.

1979   **261**

US President Jimmy Carter and First Secretary of the Central Committee of the Communist Party of the USSR Leonid Brezhnev sign the SALT II disarmament treaty. Soviet troops intervene in Afghanistan. Poland endures the 'winter of the century'. John Paul II makes his first pilgrimage to the Polish People's Republic.

1980   **322**

The 22nd Olympic Games are held in Moscow and boycotted by some capitalist countries. Strikes break out in Poland's coastal shipyards. 'Solidarity' is born as an independent, self-governing trade union. Protesters from the Interfactory Strike Commission issue the authorities with twenty-one demands, including petitions about the Church. Designed by Philip Johnson and John Burgee, the Crystal Cathedral, Garden Grove, California, is completed.

1981 437

The First Congress of the Solidarity Trade Union begins and the weekly paper Solidarność (Solidarity) starts publication. Solidarity leaders, led by Lech Wałęsa, are given an audience with Pope John Paul II. Cardinal Wyszyński dies. The funeral is a demonstration of religious and patriotic sentiment. Martial law is introduced in Poland. Due to problems with supply, the government introduces food ration cards.

1982 604

In Poland, food prices increase on average by 241 per cent. The state intensifies its control over society and its monopoly of power. Solidarity is made illegal, and the Association of Polish Journalists and the Union of Polish Stage Actors are dissolved. The authorities announce their decision to build a metro in Warsaw.

1983 741

Lech Wałęsa receives the Nobel Prize in Stockholm. The government abolishes martial law after 586 days. John Paul II makes a second pilgrimage to Poland.

1984 812

The AT&T building in Manhattan, designed by Philip Johnson, is opened.

1985 863

Mikhail Gorbachev becomes Secretary of the Central Committee of the Communist Party of the Soviet Union. The Hong Kong & Shanghai Bank, designed by Norman Foster and colleagues, opens in Hong Kong.

1986 890

The USSR admits that there has been a disaster at the Chernobyl nuclear power plant. Construction is completed on the London headquarters of Lloyd's Register, designed by Richard Rogers.

1987   **858**

Pope John Paul II visits Poland for the third time. US Vice-President George Bush meets with Solidarity leader Lech Wałęsa during his visit to Poland. The IBA (International Construction Exhibition) is held in West Berlin.

1988   **856**

In Poland, the Act on the Freedom of Economic Activity comes into force.

1989   **865**

Solidarity is officially declared legal, again. A series of laws on commercializing industrial enterprises and establishing private companies is approved. The Polish Round Table Talks are conducted between the government and the opposition in Warsaw. The first, partly free, elections to the Sejm are held. The opposition wins over sixty per cent of the votes. State socialism ends in Poland.

Rural and urban areas and the number of churches built

Between 1945 and 1989, there were two 'waves' of church construction. The first one took place during the period of the Thaw following the death of Joseph Stalin. As a result of several years of political liberalization, more than a hundred churches were built. At that time, small and medium-size buildings were erected, mainly in villages, where the power of the socialist state over space was relatively limited. The second, larger wave began after the economic crisis of the second half of the 1970s, the election of Karol Wojtyła to the Papacy, and the mass strikes organized by Solidarity. During this time, buildings of various sizes were erected, both in cities and in villages, throughout the entire country. To a broad extent the churches were erected by the first generation of urban proletarians. While in 1945 two-thirds of Poles lived in villages, in 1980 these proportions were reversed.

Author: Tomasz Świetlik

Data sources: Index of Parishes in Poland, data as of 31 December 2015, Institute for Catholic Church Statistics, Warsaw 2006; Day-VII Architecture project database

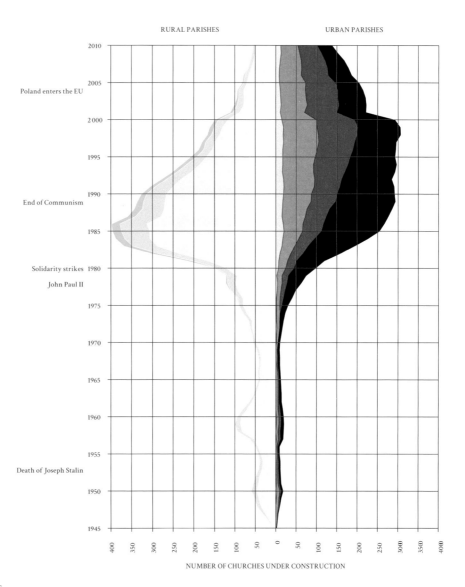

RURAL PARISHES   URBAN PARISHES

2010
2005
Poland enters the EU
2000
1995
1990
End of Communism
1985
Solidarity strikes 1980
John Paul II
1975
1970
1965
1960
1955
Death of Joseph Stalin
1950
1945

400 350 300 250 200 150 100 50   0   50 100 150 200 250 300 350 400

NUMBER OF CHURCHES UNDER CONSTRUCTION

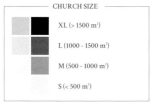

CHURCH SIZE

XL (> 1500 m²)

L (1000 - 1500 m²)

M (500 - 1000 m²)

S (< 500 m²)

Catholic churches built in Poland since 1945

Author: Szymon Pifczyk

Data source: Day-VII Architecture, project database

• A post-war church

◯ A church, which you will find in this book

INTERVIEWS WITH ARCHITECTS

Context

Interview with Marian Tunikowski

Wrocław, 7 October 2016

In Eastern Bloc countries, all architectural work was centralized in large design offices. This was logical within a command economy: consolidating architectural offices made it possible to implement its first five-year plan more efficiently. To a certain extent, architects also benefited from this situation: working in a vast conglomerate provided them with contacts and networking experience and access to technology, enabling professional development. However, at the same time the profession became industrialized, so that architects were ulti-mately reduced to mere cogs in the great machine of state-controlled design and construction.

Gradually losing all prospect of finding self-fulfilment in planning offices, architects searched for it elsewhere. The only two 'escape routes' available to them were either to enter the occasional competitions for public buildings or else to design churches for the only other large, non-state investor – the Catholic Church. Over time, two parallel worlds emerged. By day, architects planned large prefabricated housing estates deprived of churches for ideological reasons. By night, they devoted their spare time to realizing their creative ambitions by designing the 'missing' churches.

Izabela Cichońska: What was Miastoprojekt (City-Project) and what did your work there involve?
Marian Tunikowski: The full name was: Biuro Projektowo-Badawcze Budown-ictwa Ogólnego, Miastoprojekt-Wrocław (Design and Research Office of General Building, the City-Project Wrocław). It was a kind of conglomerate. In its heyday, it had 850 employees, 650 of whom were working on architectural design. The office was fully self-sufficient, with separate vertical departments – design, administra-tion and service. The first vertical department consisted of general construction and specialist studios. The general construction studio consisted of architectural, construction, installation, electrical, telecommunications and cost estimation teams. Apart from that, the Miastoprojekt had its own technical library and an entire subdivision dedicated to the copying, binding and sending of documentation to the ordering party. Today, in the digital era, it is difficult to imagine the rooms full of heliographic copiers, in which everything, including reproduced documen-tation, was permeated with ammonia, or the 'typewriters hall', in which about

twenty typists typed up manuscripts of the descriptive sections for each project. The hall was as noisy as the halls of weaving plants – it was quite difficult to bear.

For a young architect, the office was a great place for one's development and there were plenty of people to learn from. At that time, private design offices did not exist. Following graduation, you could work only in a state-run office. Ours employed a number of designers and experts of various specialities, all of them experienced professionals. Before leaving the studio, each project was discussed at a so-called technical board that convened the best architects and specialists.

At what point in your professional career did you get the opportunity to design a church?
My father was asked to design a church in Świdnica [a city in south-western Poland] and he suggested that I should also put a design forward. So, two designs were created: my father's and mine. Both of them were exhibited in the form of mock-ups; after public discussion, my project was chosen by the residents of the housing estate and by the church authorities. The building permit was issued in 1982, when I was twenty seven. That year I was also granted my architectural licence. I began working on the church with many reservations, but also with great enthusiasm.

Could you describe the urban context of this project?
My father, who was mainly involved in urban planning, created the layout of Osiedle Młodych [Housing Estate of the Young] in the 1970s. Urban planning was his passion, and many housing estates were built according to his designs in Lower Silesia. Osiedle Młodych has an unambiguous, closed spatial arrangement. Following years of efforts by church authorities and residents, the state finally agreed to a parish church in the area. The proposed location for the church, namely at the edge of the estate and the highest point of the area, led to a planning problem. The site for the church fell between a long block of flats and allotment gardens. This position would have made it difficult to establish a proper spatial relation with the surrounding buildings. However, the force of my father's arguments resulted in permission being granted to introduce changes to the urban layout of the buildings already under construction. The construction process of one of the buildings was stopped – luckily at foundation stage. This is how the inner space between the buildings was opened up, connecting the area with the site where the church was to be built. The entire matter required great negotiation skills, especially in the context of building a church and the political dimension of doing so at the time. However, the negotiations were successful in the end. Had the construction of the residential part been more advanced at that point, this change wouldn't have been possible and today's church and its surroundings would look completely different. After a time, the building of the church got underway and

Church of Our Lady Queen of Poland, Świdnica

architect: Marian Tunikowski
construction dates: 1982-2001
GPS: 50.85, 16.4655

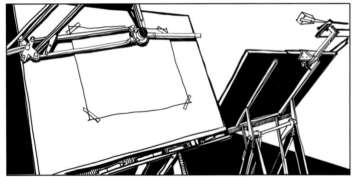

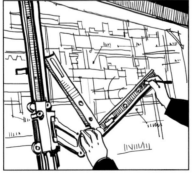

the topic of land use in this new urban area came up again at Miastoprojekt, and I was assigned to work on it.

You were a sort of 'double agent'?

When designing this church, I worked two shifts – during the day I was at the office, at night I was working on the church [laughter]. The matter of the estate and its development belonged to Miastoprojekt. Because the urban layout changed, the issue returned to the drawing board. This time, mine. Some problems arose when designing this urban space. Initially, I wanted to situate a street on the axis of the church's main entrance, between the surrounding buildings, but I didn't get permission from the authorities. I went straight to the mayor of Świdnica and it turned out that for political reasons it was deemed unacceptable for 'a road to lead straight to the church'. As a result, the road was moved to the side, and I designed a pedestrian route in its place. Today, I think that this solution, although shaped by political pressure, paradoxically turned out to be spatially better.

What did the design phase and the construction work involve?

Being part of Miastoprojekt and dealing with industrialized construction methods, I never thought that an object of such scale could be built, let's say, in a cost-effective way. We never imagined that we wouldn't be able to take advantage of the technologies available at the time. One of the stages of the design process involved preparing guidelines for investment. This document defined how, using which methods, and with what kind of equipment the subsequent building stages would be carried out. Naturally, we assumed that a professional team would carry out the construction of the building with the use of a crane. Imagine our surprise when we learned that the construction was to be carried out by the brother of the parish priest, a highlander who arrived with a team consisting of several of his mates. At the meeting, it turned out that we could forget about the crane – too expensive. And indeed, this church emerged from a forest of timber scaffolding – just like in the Middle Ages. The force behind the construction was the local parish and especially the parish priest, who had an ability to acquire 'unobtainable' building materials that were beyond all price at the time.

Thanks to people who had jobs in various industrial plants in Świdnica, we were also able to get the professional support we needed for the construction. For instance, the steel structure of the roof, which has a surface area of 3,500 m², was created in Wagony Świdnica, the rail-freight wagons factory.

The permanent construction team, including the foreman, consisted of no more than six or seven people. Everyone else working on the site were a part of the levée en masse initiated by the parish priest. These people came to work following each Sunday's pastoral announcements. There were about twenty-thousand people in the parish, and a lot of them were able to help with the construction by contributing their labour, either professional or physical. However, their work had to be organized and managed. Just imagine that every day between 100-150 people arrived at the construction site not knowing what they would do that day. Most of them had no practical experience in construction work. However, thanks to the foreman's organizational skills, the "mass levy" turned out to be an efficient strategy, and its progress could be seen daily.

The entire reinforced concrete structure was erected without the use of a single crane or concrete pump. The construction site had two concrete mixers in constant operation. The concrete was poured into wheelbarrows that were elevated as high as ten metres using many small, sloped wooden ramps. Then a construction hoist was used to erect the central tower, enabling the wheelbarrows to be pulled up even higher. The building is not only very tall – the crucifix-shaped tower is seventy-metres high – but also goes deep underground. In one part of the building, the cellars are about five metres deep for a very prosaic reason – the basement had to accommodate the then-modern ventilation fans.

On this construction site I found out what a szlauchwaga was. This very simple levelling device, a rubber hose filled with water with glass tubes on each end, was used daily by the construction team. As it turned out later on, the professional theodolite measurements taken by surveyors detected only two-millimetre deviations in levels at measuring points over a range of 80 metres. Later, we joked that the surveyors came to the construction site to check the accuracy of their theodolite using the foreman's water-level device [laughs].

So, you were lucky to have a very meticulous construction team?
Yes, so much so that it led to one, quite unfortunate incident. I came to the construction site and noticed a big inconsistency from the drawings. On the clinker brick façade of the chapel, two additional concrete beams appeared to have been added. When I saw this, I immediately asked the foreman for an explanation. Calmly, he replied: 'We followed the drawing to the letter!'… It was simply bad luck: the adhesive tape on the torn tracing paper from which the copy was taken caused a shadow to appear on the diazo copy of the drawing. The shadow appeared in a place and of a size that it could have actually seemed part of the original plan. And they did indeed follow the plan to the letter, in good faith. ∎

Marian Tunikowski (b. 1955) — Architect, and graduate of Wrocław University of Science and Technology, Tunikowski founded the Design and Execution Services Studio Mat-Projekt, where he currently works. He has designed numerous plans for multi- and single-family residential buildings, as well as public utility buildings and automotive facilities. He designed the Church of the Blessed Virgin Mary, Queen of Poland, in Świdnica.

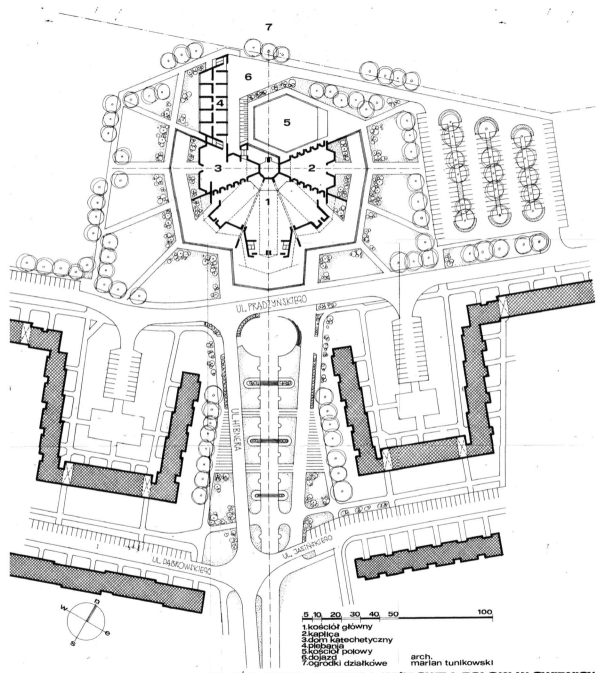

1. kościół główny
2. kaplica
3. dom katechetyczny
4. plebania
5. kościół polowy
6. dojazd
7. ogródki działkowe

arch.
marian tunikowski

ARAFIALNY ZESPÓŁ SAKRALNY P/W MATKI BOSKIEJ KRÓLOWEJ POLSKI W ŚWIDNICY

Original designs of the Church of Our Lady Queen of Poland, courtesy of Marian Tunikowski

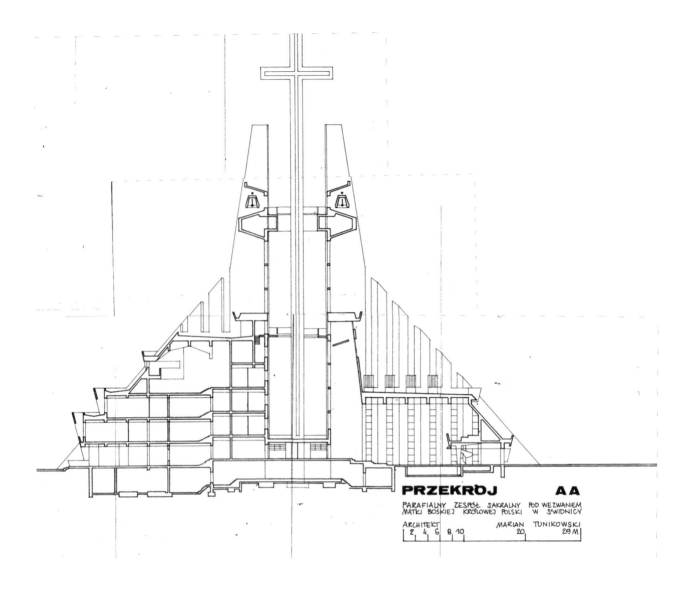

PRZEKRÓJ **A A**

PARAFIALNY ZESPÓŁ SAKRALNY POD WEZWANIEM
MATKI BOSKIEJ KRÓLOWEJ POLSKI W ŚWIDNICY

ARCHITEKT MARIAN TUNIKOWSKI
2 4 6 8 10 20 29 M

Original designs of the Church of Our Lady Queen of Poland, courtesy of Marian Tunikowski

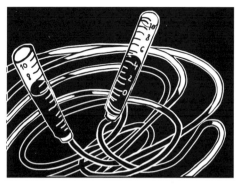
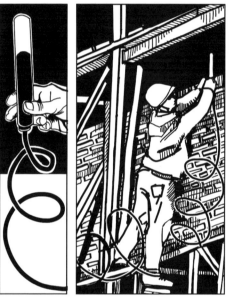

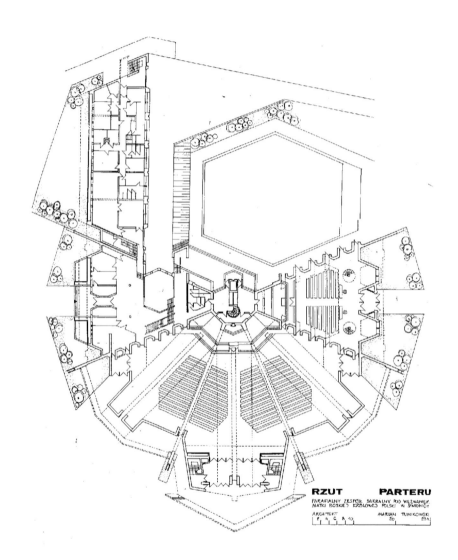

RZUT   PARTERU

PARAFIALNY ZESPÓŁ SAKRALNY POD WEZWANIEM
MATKI BOSKIEJ KRÓLOWEJ POLSKI W ŚWIDNICY

ARCHITEKT: MARIAN TUNIKOWSKI

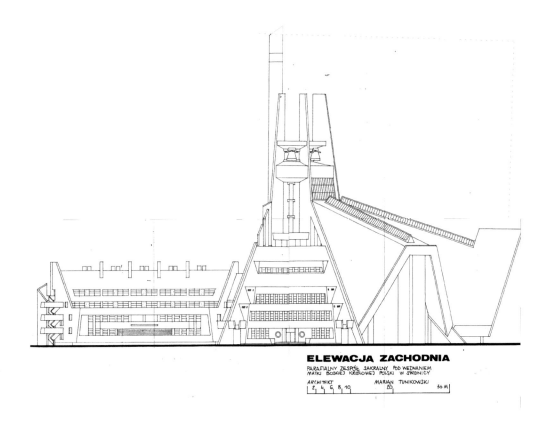

ELEWACJA ZACHODNIA
PARAFIALNY ZESPÓŁ SAKRALNY POD WEZWANIEM
MATKI BOSKIEJ KRÓLOWEJ POLSKI W ŚWIDNICY
ARCHITEKT   MARIAN TUNIKOWSKI

Original designs of the Church of Our Lady Queen of Poland, courtesy of Marian Tunikowski

Collaboration

Interview with Stanislaw Niemczyk

Tychy, 20 May 2016

In response to the challenges of modern times, the Catholic Church called the Second Vatican Council (1962-65). Liturgy was the focus of its reform. In terms of architecture, this heralded dramatic spatial changes, beginning with the positioning of the altar and a transforming of the spatial relationship between priest and worshippers. Over the following decade, hundreds of new church projects were developed in France, Italy and other Western Catholic countries. In those projects, the notion of 'community' promoted by the Council was most often made manifest in the floor plan of churches, in which the celebrant was placed among the congregation.

In Poland, behind the Iron Curtain, it was far more difficult to introduce these conciliar changes. Contacts with the Vatican were complicated and sporadic, and there was no way to dispel doubts immediately as to how to interpret the Council's guidelines. The architects sought new solutions independently. Stanislaw Niemczyk, the architect of five churches, developed a unique design method. By involving the congregation in the process of creating the church, he built a community at the same time.

Kuba Snopek: How did the Church of the Holy Spirit in Tychy come about?
Stanisław Niemczyk: In the 1970s, the political authorities of the PRL approved the construction of a number of new churches. At the time, Tychy had only two sacred buildings for eighty-thousand people. The town obtained permission for one new church.

The priest appointed by the bishop came into the state design office and was directed to me. Once I began working on the design, I met with the parish priest quite frequently. Since there was no textbook for building churches, he had to precisely define the needs and functions of the new building. At that time, the Council resolutions concerning the interior space of churches had just come into force and involved a radical change in the relationship between worshippers and priest. This encouraged a new outlook – an official stance on the Council resolutions hadn't been yet worked out.

The concept for the church was therefore based on the post-conciliar ideas of liturgy: the place of sacrifice had to be located at the centre of the church, with worshippers facing it on all four sides. The community now surrounded the altar, because there is no stronger power in the Church than the Eucharist. We may have frescoes that are as beautiful as that of the Sistine Chapel, but they will never constitute the essence of Faith. The Eucharist is the main element that provides strength and power. Otherwise there would be no point in building a church. Should a church be built merely for the frescoes, statues or stained-glass windows?

When I designed the Tychy church, the Old Testament was the most important point of reference. What was the meaning of a church back then? The Old Testament clearly describes God's tabernacle and the sacred abode of the saints, beginning with the space itself through the furniture, utensils, liturgical equipment and lighting. This, in my opinion, belonged to the highest rank of the material world that I could reproduce. There was quality in it, because even a stone contains the element of creation. I wanted the abode of God to remain central, of utmost importance. The second prominent element was the light shown to man by God, which symbolizes the descent of the Holy Spirit.

I always try to get to the heart of the matter. This is why I could never design a mosque. Knowing Islam only superficially, I would never agree to such a task – or I would be doing what the socialist realists did, when they were forced to design architecture they did not believe in.

The essence of the Church is the Eucharist, the transformation that takes place at the altar. If you don't take this truth as a starting point, you would simply have to work backwards. How should a modern church look? Ought it to be built of brick? Of stone? But these are the wrong kinds of questions. Churches can be built of wood, stone or brick, and if someone asked me to build one of straw, I would as long as I understood the meaning of this concept. From the religious point of view, the building's appearance is never decisive. I am not interested in any museums – the Church is a living organism. It cannot be subject to the vicissitudes of the authorities; it exists regardless of the comings and goings of bishops and popes. The Church is a Church from the moment of Jesus Christ's death and resurrection. Regardless of whether it is a community of two, twenty or two-thousand people, its essence is the mystery of the Transfiguration. The value of a church is determined by what is happening inside it at any given moment. And what happens, happens only with the participation of the priest and the faithful present in it – this is the main relationship. If the architect cannot grasp this, then the outcome of his work can only ever be entirely artificial. Despite all its specific and modern qualities, such a building will not possess an ounce of genuineness. Only when a church becomes the beating heart of a community of parishioners, is it truly a church. End of story.

Church of the Holy Spirit, Tychy

architect: Stanisław Niemczyk
construction dates: 1978-1982
GPS: 50.1066, 18.9658

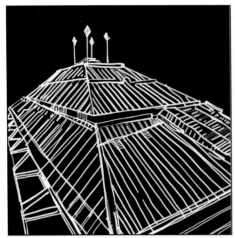

Did the parishioners take part in the construction of the church in Tychy?
The Polish People's Republic lacked materials for everything: factories, houses, etc. To build a church we had to organize our own so-called DIY method. We had to work in the afternoons, arrange materials in one way or another, and rely on the help of volunteers and parishioners. People wanted to help – there was a great willingness to help, to act. The parish priest rallied these people by announcing the construction work from the pulpit – everyone knew that the construction work was underway. Some people came and said: 'Father, I can come and help', 'I can work with concrete', 'I can work with wood', and so on. The parish priest would go to people's homes during his pastoral visits, and so he knew who was an engineer, who was a carpenter, and so on, and that was a great help. Some days, as many as forty people would turn up to work on the site. They would come before or after work, they would work in shifts. Saturdays weren't free back then, and miners had to work on Sundays as well – please remember that.

Some people helped out of the goodness of their hearts. They wanted to build a church that they and their children could use. Others helped because they felt the need to identify with what they deemed a worthy cause. They truly did their best, sharing their skills with one another. It was fantastic. For me, however, this way of working was absolutely nothing new. After the war, my parents had to help rebuild the local school with their own hands just so I could get an education. Of course there weren't any funds or materials for that. They had to use whatever was available. This is the spirit in which I was raised.

At one point, we needed concrete for these large, 1.2 metre high frames requiring one cubic metre of concrete. Back then, a cement mixer could hold a maximum of six cubic metres, i.e. enough for about five metres. Meanwhile, we needed concrete for almost sixty metres of framing. The priest ordered the concrete legally, submitting an application. After two or three cement mixers the state company called saying there would be no more concrete deliveries. Accordingly, the priest made some phone calls to his parishioners. In the past, each household in Poland had a concrete mixer made of a bicycle wheel and a barrel. People ran around the neighbourhood and searched for them. In no time at all, a dozen or so of such concrete mixers were in rotation on the construction site. From dawn till dusk, we carried concrete in buckets until we managed to finish the frame.

We acquired the bricks in batches. I am very fond of brick; it was used as a building material where I grew up. All brickyards in the PRL were state-run; there weren't any private ones. The centralized economy meant that one had to apply to the ministry to get an allocated amount. Each brickyard had a different production method, so I had to meticulously examine the material provided by each parishioner. To build houses, people burned bricks themselves or tried to source them wherever possible – you'd get one allocation from Lublin and then another from

53

Lower Silesia. It was possible to get five to ten thousand bricks from the state. People took some for their own needs and some to the church. There was no point in hoping that all these bricks would be the same. I got one kind for the presbytery and another kind for another part of the church.

The church in Czechowice-Dziedzice was built after the fall of communism, but it was also community built....

When the initial idea was developed, the priest proposed that the Church project be exhibited during the Lenten retreats. First, all parishioners would go, and then women, men, and young people would attend separately. I brought in the mock-up and persuaded the parishioners to take part in the construction.

The construction took two years, which was a great effort. Every day, forty men worked on the construction site, volunteering with great joy. We would work in pouring rain or scorching heat. Women would make coffee and cake for 9:00 a.m. and we would sit down under the cross and eat. At noon, lunch was prepared for the second shift. Each evening at home, I'd prepare several drawings, and at 6:00 a.m. the priest would come pick me up in his car, and we'd drive to the construction site. I'd stay all day, adjusting plans with the bricklayers on the go. The priest says that to this day he has no idea how we managed to complete and open a new church in only two years. The parishioners, six-hundred families, contributed their own resources. There were enough funds leftover for the church bells and paintings.

And how about the Franciscan church that is currently being built next door to your house?

From the very beginning, picnics and festivals were held at the building site and in the park next door. Once the construction work began, nativity scenes with animals were arranged as an excuse for people to visit with their entire families. There even was a bonfire, with sausages and all – hundreds of people came with their children. We have been building this church for fifteen years now. At first, we had more people from the parish coming in to help out, but now we live in a free-market economy, people have to earn their living. As a society, we now function differently, we have different family relationships. Our society used to be very resilient. At the moment, the dominant attitude is: I don't have time, I cannot make it, call me later.

How much physical labour have you done in your life? The toil, the sweat, the getting so fed up with it at the end of the day that you ask yourself: 'What on God's Earth have I done to deserve this?' I have done a lot of hard labour in my life, both out of goodwill and out of necessity. But I value such work highly and I would recommend it to everyone. One cannot compare jogging around the city in a tracksuit with one's headphones on with what we are talking about here – which is to say valuable, necessary work, work that benefits others as well. ∎

Stanisław Niemczyk (b. 1943 — † 2019) — Architect and winner of the 1998 SARP Honorary Award, Niemczyk graduated from Kraków University of Technology. After graduating, he was involved in Miastoprojekt Tychy (City-Project, Tychy) designing residential and commercial buildings. He has designed five churches, including the Church of the Holy Spirit, in Tychy. He runs his own studio in the city.

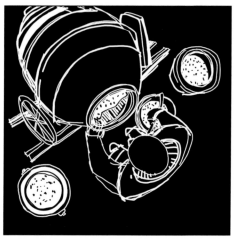
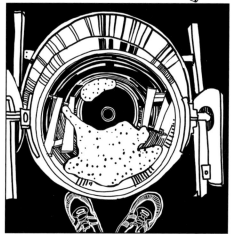

Church of Jesus Christ the Redeemer, Czechowice-Dziedzice

architect: Stanisław Niemczyk
construction dates: 1995-1998
GPS: 49.8872, 19.0256

Church of Divine Mercy, Kraków

architects: Stanisław Niemczyk, Marek Kuszewski
construction dates: 1991-2000
GPS: 50.0694, 19.9611

Church of St Francis of Assisi and St Clare, Tychy

architect: Stanisław Niemczyk
construction dates: 2000-under construction
GPS: 50.1052, 19.0019

Politics

Interview with Romuald Loegler

Krakow, 26 April 2016

Throughout the entire period of the PRL's existence, state and church institutions functioned side by side. They both had their own administrations, institutions and experts. State and Church authorities constantly competed with each other and, in various ways, sought support from society. Decisions concerning the construction of new churches were based on political, rather than spatial considerations. Prohibited up until Joseph Stalin's death, new church constructions boomed in the short period of the Thaw. Then, banned by the state during the 1960s, they reappeared during the rule of the so-called pragmatists in the following decade. The breakthrough, however, came with the election of Cardinal Karol Wojtyła to the Papacy in 1978. Wojtyła, a fervent participant in the construction works while still a cardinal, continued his support for church builders when he became Pope. Two years later, the church building boom began and the politicization of churches was reflected in their architecture: they gained additional cultural functions, catechetical rooms and served as meeting places for the political opposition.

Kuba Snopek: Please tell us about the construction of the Church of St. Jadwiga Holy Queen of Poland, in Kraków.

Romuald Loegler: The political background to the construction process was problematic. The cardinal at the time, Karol Wojtyła, and his successor, Franciszek Macharski, very much wanted to build this church. Wojtyła fought to secure the good location. He argued to the authorities that if they wished to avoid civil unrest of the kind that took place in Nowa Huta in 1960, they had better agree. In his correspondence with the local first secretary, the future Pope wrote: 'I leave the issue of location to the secretary's consideration. I can no longer influence the will of the parishioners. Should this lead to a conflict, please assume all responsibility.'

Eventually, the secretary at the time granted permission and building work began. The other location proposed by the party turned out to be just a vulgar ploy. The authorities wanted to force us to accept to build under a high-voltage power line. They pushed us to accept an area next to a newly designed tram route which had a high-voltage line that would serve as a power source for trams. If we'd accepted we would have had to pay for the cabling and it would've been a financial catastrophe. Eventually, however, we were able to erect the church on a lot that had been designated for a cultural centre. The church argued that there was already a housing estate – a prefabricated blocks of flats – there and that thanks to this investment the area would gain access to culture and sport, a school and a religious building. Indeed, today there is a theatre, sports fields and an indoor gym. The sports hall is in the basement of the church, below the crypt – this was not part of the original design. The theatre hall is located in the so-called former lower church situated below the main nave. It has all the amenities you need to organize art exhibitions and music concerts. It also has a school.

We designed our church bearing in mind the appearance of the nearby housing estate. It seemed to me that anything with a hint of a regional flavour was entirely out of the question. The opinion-forming committee rated the project highly, but said that it wasn't suitable for this area, for the city. I also had a second project, an even more scenographic and theatrical one. It would have been a little more expensive to build, but in my opinion even more attractive. Their reaction was difficult – 'Very good for a world exhibition of architecture, but not for here'. We were not given the green light to begin construction.

So, I went to speak with Cardinal Wojtyła before he departed for his first conclave. We talked for an hour. That seems a short time, but it's a lot when it came to him. He was an educated man, a sensitive man, a poet and a playwright, a man dedicated to the theatre. We talked about the scenography of the project, the storyline that would, consciously, prepare worshippers for celebrating the mass. We talked about how the Church's language must move closer to that of contemporary society, must be made more understandable. We decided that no shortcuts, no sentimental returns to historical models would make the slightest sense. We shared the view that we were building a church in keeping with the development of civilization, instead of hanging onto traditional models. I presented him both projects, their mock-ups, and told him about the external opinions I received. The cardinal asked me a few questions and said: 'You do know that we will build it, right? And he pointed to the draft the committee rejected for being 'too bold'.

The result of the meeting was positive, because when Wojtyła said that something had to be built, it had to be built. Later, during the construction work, I would take the bus that passed by the site and I could overhear what people were saying about the church then under construction. The opinions were damning. They savaged it. In 1988, the church was officially consecrated. During his homily, John Paul II, of course, referred to the church and he said: 'We have a new cathedral in Kraków'. The next day, I got on the same bus and all I could hear were enthusiastic opinions' [laughter].

Church of Holy Queen Jadwiga, Kraków

architects: Romuald Loegler, Jacek Czekaj
construction dates: 1979-1988
GPS: 50.0842, 19.9235

This was the second building in Kraków to be designed with a textured concrete façade. I wanted to restore a human face to concrete, so that it wouldn't seem such an 'anti-human' material. I was taught that it is not necessary for the consistent execution of a good idea to rely exclusively on modern construction methods, that such can be achieved by drawing on traditional knowledge. The elements had to be completed as simply and efficiently as possible. Their texture came from a timber formwork – people from the highlands constructed it; they could do anything in wood. It was crucial for the formwork to be solid. No curving or bending could be tolerated – especially, as these constituted the load-bearing walls supporting the cantilever slabs.

In terms of square meterage, the building turned out to be huge – this was in keeping with the trend at the time to build upper and lower churches. We had to ensure we had room for worshippers from the neighbouring parish in case they couldn't obtain a building permit for their church. Later, after Poland's transformation [from socialism to capitalism], I adapted the lower church into a theatre. ■

Dr Romuald Loegler (b. 1940) — Architect, Loegler completed his doctoral thesis at Warsaw University of Technology. In the 1970s, he did an apprenticeship at Karl Schwanzer's studio in Vienna. He is the co-founder of the Architecture Biennale in Kraków, and former editor-in-chief of Architekt (Architect) magazine. In 1987, together with his partners, he opened a private architectural studio.

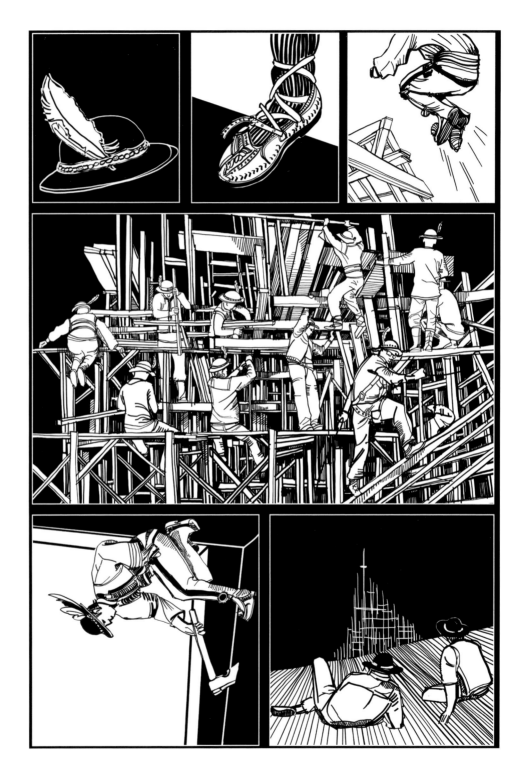

Church of the Immaculate Heart of Mary, Częstochowa

architect: Romuald Loegler
construction dates: 2005-under construction
GPS: 50.8181, 19.2038

Theatre

Interview with Jerzy Gurawski

Poznań, 20 May 2016

In the mid-twentieth century, the burgeoning popularity of cinema and television presented both Church and theatre with similar challenges. To hold on to their audiences, both needed to reorganize and adapt to the rapidly changing world. Interestingly, Church and theatre reformers often reached similar conclusions. Jerzy Grotowski, while establishing his experimental 'Laboratorium'(Laboratory) theatre, proposed to rid theatre of unnecessary elements and instead focus on the relationship between audience and actors. He questioned notions of 'rich' theatre. At the same time, the reforms of the Second Vatican Council urged the Church to make the liturgy easier to understand and to simplify church interiors.

The flow of design ideas between churches and theatres was occasionally reciprocal. Grotowski often drew on Christian tradition, while Jerzy Gurawski, Grotowski's long-time collaborator and architect of his theatrical space, passed on the solutions developed in the Laboratory theatre to his Church of the Blessed Virgin Mary, Queen of Poland, in Głogów.

Karolina Popera: How did the church in Głogów come about?
Jerzy Grotowski brought me in from Kraków, where I had settled after the war. I created the space for each of his shows. I learned to move in theatre space – not in a strictly architectural sense, but rather in an intimate way, in association with ideas. In such a space, magic and mystery really can emerge.

Thanks to a friend, I was commissioned to design a church in Głogów. The town was expanding rapidly at the time on the back of a discovery of copper deposits. Many people moved there – mostly farmers, who suddenly found themselves in town and became miners. On the one hand, it was quite nice – all things considered, such people did earn a decent living. On the other hand, however, it was a little dreadful. Once these farmers had had fields, forests, cows mooing at them, and now they spent entire days underground, surrounded by grime and darkness. The audience for whom I was supposed to design the space was therefore quite unusual.

The other fantastic thing was the Second Vatican Council's reformulation of the principles for designing churches. At one point, the Vatican's guidelines coincided with the views of people such as Grotowski and myself. Old rules and established patterns were abolished. The theatre that we opened, together with Grotowski, moved away from a traditionally, or even centrally, located stage towards a more open performance space. Every single thing in his theatre was mystical and all the melodies and singing referred to the liturgy. This was most clearly visible in Akropolis [Acropolis] – a play about Auschwitz, about the Holocaust. The performance ended with the prisoners carrying the figure of Christ and singing. Until very recently, this singing still came vividly to mind – funeral, liturgical, simply unbelievable. Almost every one of his plays contained some religion-related features, and not always Christian ones. He was able to depict this very well.

The Church, meanwhile, abolished Latin as its official language and the liturgy became easily understandable to all churchgoers. The old patterns and their spatial rules were removed from churches. Suddenly it was possible to have a centralized layout with the altar in the middle, around which the worshippers gathered. The priest now had to stand at the entrance and greet everyone. It was recommended to place the holy sacrament to one side, rather than at the back. Suddenly, churches no longer needed to be designed within that old, ossified framework. This was a lot of fun. The Vatican Council also abolished the inclusion of separate chapels, but priests were very used to having them. However, I took some liberties and looked for inspiration from the design of amphitheatres, designing a chapel that was connected to the entire interior via arcades. When I had this idea, I was happy as a flea in the doghouse! This shift from a Latin cross to an amphitheatre! This truly opened up church space.

Among the things I was fascinated with were low arcades supported by pillars and covered with a single sloped roof – the essential elements of churches in what used to be eastern Poland. This is where people would hang out before or after mass, talk to their friends and neighbours, make plans to go and have a drink together. It was a place where one could come close to the sacred, but not be right in the middle of it. And to this day, people just love to hang out outside churches. And that's why we included these arcades. Moreover, since I was fascinated by the design of Gothic churches, my buttresses refer to buildings from that period.

You followed the Vatican Council's guidelines, but what inspired you?
The Council's guidelines allowed us to experiment with the space. Romanesque churches are beautiful – they consist of boulders, a wooden roof truss and nothing else. The light falls in through small openings. The wood in those churches fascinated me. At the time, the tendency was to build churches in concrete. That was considered modern, so everyone designed in concrete. However, the acoustics in them were terrible – voices would echo and bounce around, especially in churches with long naves. When I was working on the design, I thought I should somehow try to muffle the church interior. And it turns out that the interior, which we built with laminated wood beams and wooden lining, has excellent acoustics. No hard

materials were used; everything was sculpted, giving the sound a perfect reflection and breakdown. The acoustics in the church in Głogów are so good that a priest with a well-trained voice can speak normally without needing a microphone. When the organ was installed, the pastor invited an outstanding soprano to sing, and they performed Ave Maria. I am usually quite cynical and sceptical about life, but even I got goosebumps. The church was completely full and everyone fell completely silent – there was only the singer with her wonderful voice… Holy Mary! That was a blast.

How were the details of the project agreed?
In those days everything was extremely simple. We created a design concept and the Curia accepted it immediately. We gained access to the site in no time. All the PZPR first secretaries in towns such as Głogów were deeply religious, and became party secretaries just for the sake of having a career. Their main aspiration was to remain close to the Church, so that their children could be baptized and have church weddings, which is something that the damned party wouldn't officially allow. These first secretaries had to have good connections with the priests so that they would receive this service on the quiet. The priests naturally baptized the children and administered sacraments to them – making out as if nothing had ever happened. As a result, they had no problems obtaining permits.

Izabela Cichońska: What shape did the construction process take?
It was fantastic! Those were extraordinary times. The idea was that the church would stand out from among blocks of flats. Everyone eagerly awaited its construction. Local residents had great respect for the parish priest and when he invited them all to cooperate, they were happy to come and work. Of course, there was also a professional team with the appropriate knowledge and building skills. But there were also the parishioners, people who worked in the mines. They were used to physical labour, they knew how to do it very well. This church was built by the entire community.

Did parishioners try to acquire building materials on their own?
For fear of being struck by lightning, no one would dream of stealing materials from the church construction site. It was rather the other way around – all the directors, such as the director of the copper smelter that manufactured metal sheets, wholeheartedly supported the construction. The parish priest was on friendly terms with all of them; he baptized their children and grandchildren in secret. When sheet metal was needed, they arranged for it to be delivered. The entire church is covered with copper sheeting that was otherwise almost unobtainable at the time. The same goes for the internal construction. It is supported on glued laminated timber beams. Together with the parish priest, we managed to get some from a

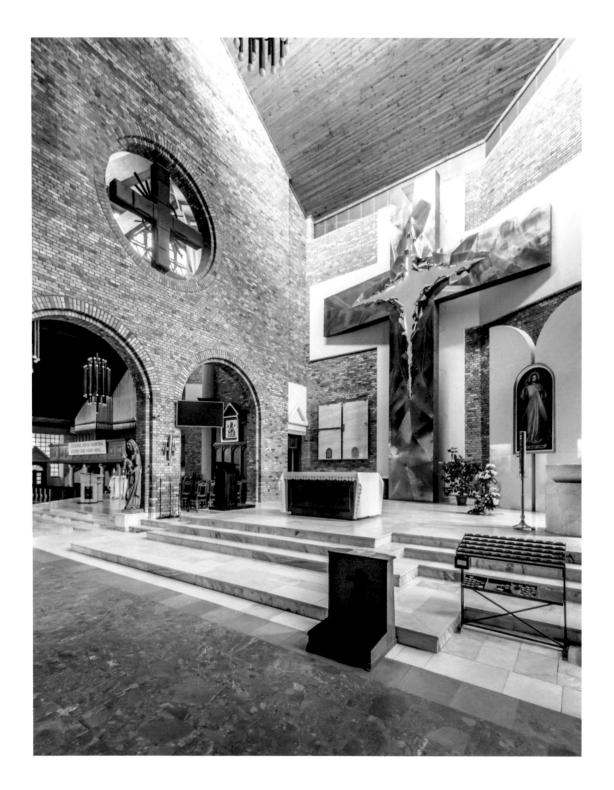

factory located 280 kilometres away. They arrived on special platforms imported from Sweden and were designed in such a way that the trusses could move around, overhang, on a sharp turn. They had to be delivered at night, when there was no traffic and the streets could be closed.

Karolina Popera: Do you see any far-reaching differences in the building of churches from the 1970s, the 1980s and the first decade of the twenty-first century?

The earlier churches were built with the help of local communities, using DIY methods; this amateurism lends them a certain charm. What can I say – back then, a concrete wall would still have the marks of the scaffolding boards and grain of the wood; it wouldn't be exactly straight. Nowadays, this kind of thing is only ever done for show – today's churches are way too polished, too hi-tech. In the past, the hard work and effort of those who took part in their construction was clearly visible. ■

Jerzy Gurawski (b. 1935) — Architect, lecturer at Poznań University of Technology, and winner of the 2007 SARP Honorary Award, Gurawski graduated from Kraków University of Technology, where he wrote his masters thesis on experimental theatre. He has worked with experimental theatre director Jerzy Grotowski on the creation of theatrical spaces. He has designed three churches, including the Church of the Blessed Virgin Mary, Queen of Poland, in Głogów.

Church of Our Lady Queen of Poland, Głogów

architects: Jerzy Gurawski, Marian Fikus
construction dates: 1981-1986
GPS: 51.6538, 16.0677

Profession

Interview with Antoni Mazur

Krakow, 26 April 2016

Antoni Mazur is the only church architect whose work spans all post-war periods. He began designing Catholic churches during the Stalinist era, and continued during the so-called period of 'little stabilization' in the 1960s and 1970s. He participated in the church construction boom of the Solidarity era and in construction during Poland's political transformation. Despite his advanced age, he continues to design.

The technological, political, legal and economic conditions may have changed, but this has not affected the exceptional consistency of his style. He has always paid great attention to the relationship between building technologies and the qualities of the building materials and architectural form. Mazur is a truly accomplished architect: he always manages to realize his ideas regardless of the limitations imposed. His career demonstrates that architecture does not have to be the outcome of external forces: sometimes the most important ingredient is the architect's own determination.

Izabela Cichońska: You have designed and built sixteen sacred buildings and taken part in the construction of a further fifty. Where did it all begin?
Antoni Mazur: My history with churches began in the winter of 1951. During the Stalinist era it was forbidden to build new churches. From time to time, however, projects related to renovations came along. My wife worked for the Polskie Pracownie Konserwacji Zabytków [State Studios for the Conservation of Cultural Property] and was commissioned by a parish priest to create a floor design. We began to work on the design together but after a time I took over this task. Back then, I would design everything in these churches and acquired many skills doing so. On construction sites I met craftsmen dealing with stone masonry, carpentry, smithery and metalwork, and I learned traditional techniques from them, gained professional knowledge. I spent hundreds of hours working and watching others work in various workshops.

I can see projects spread out on your desk. It is impressive to see a 94-year-old still working.
Of course, I am still working! At the moment I am designing the interiors of the Church of the Holy Cross and the Holy Mother of Sorrows in Dębica. I am working

on the details of the chandelier for the chapel's altar. To do this, I am using spectacles that I built myself.

For every profession involving artistic craftsmanship, the skills of the designer are crucial. The designer who entrusts a project to a sculptor or a metalworker gives up the possibility of executing it in their own way. I thus decided to master all the professions involved in artistic craftsmanship. If, for example, I came up with the idea of combining glass and metal, I would test how it worked. I would visit various glassworks, prepare drawings in 1:1 scale, build prototypes.

For the tabernacle in the Church of the Sacred Heart of Jesus in Częstochowa I developed a technique of working with melted ruby glass set directly into the metalwork. Later, I used this method to decorate chandeliers, pulpits and missals.

To finish the façade of the Church of the Holy Cross, we bought material made of a marble aggregate mixed with resin, which was then glued onto a reinforced brick grid. Thanks to this, the golden beige colour will never fade or get dirty.

When working on the tabernacle for the Church of Divine Mercy in Dębica, I figured out how to join glass and sheet metal – I poured glass over metal wire. The changes in temperature did not affect it as the pieces of wire all shrank and expanded evenly – all the more so, as it was done while hot. Then it was silver-plated.

In Częstochowa, on the façade, I used iron ore sand and granulate in the same colour from a nearby iron foundry. And all this finish is natural, no paint. It's fantastic.

The bold shape of St. Adalbert Church in Częstochowa is very impressive. Could you say a little more about its construction?

The building was meant to be two storeys high. The lower part was built in one year and was covered with a flat roof. I thought about adding double or triple diagonal buttresses in order to reduce the span. As we know, the load-bearing capacity of the beam depends on its length – the square of the span. It is calculated using particular formulas and the beam is then skilfully positioned. These beams, as well as the bent and horizontal planes, shape the roof. I was greatly impressed by the look of the fresh reinforced concrete of these pillars – before the concrete dries, it is very dark. When I went to the foundry, I noticed some black lumps of glass lying on a heap. I made sure that the priest would take all these blocks to a mill and requested that they be ground into this kind of fine particles. Then, set in a cement and glass mortar, they were glued onto the buttresses. Once that set, we rinsed it out and all that was left was the black colour. Ever since, the colour has remained the same – it isn't a painted finish, but simply black glass.

For many years, this parish, with its fifty-thousand worshippers, had been waiting for a building permit. The church got the green light after an intervention by

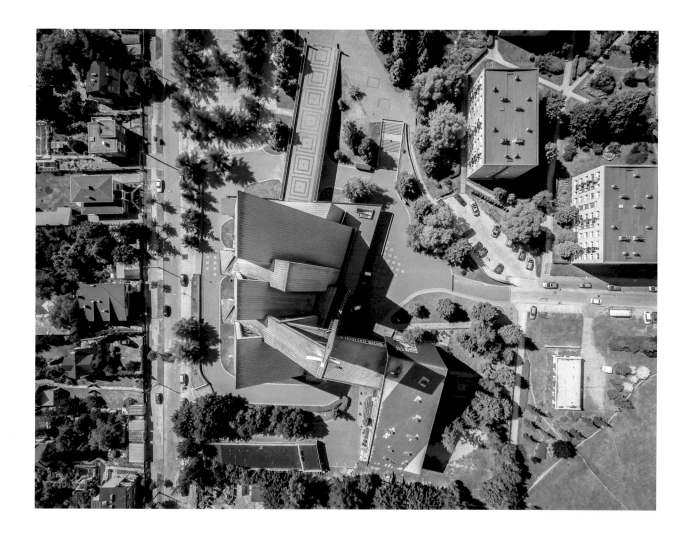

Church of St Adalbert the Bishop and Martyr, Częstochowa

architect: Antoni Mazur
construction dates: 1978-1985
GPS: 50.8325, 19.1224

Archbishop Luigi Poggi, envoy of Father Paul VI and apostolic nuncio to Poland. On top of that, the President of Częstochowa was captivated by my work. Of course he didn't show it, but he did arrange a lot for the construction site – a large land-fill site with vast differences (of up to nine metres) in terrain levels. I designed a two-storey church there. The upper church, with the assembly square, required the construction of a sixty-metre-long platform, increasing the appeal of land development on both levels. Hence, the wide stairs connecting the congregation square with its surroundings. We managed to build the lower level in one year. This was mainly due to the great foreman we had. He was able to select the right labourers and coordinated the building works very efficiently. Having good connections to the mayor, we were able to buy steel and even obtain a truss. Later on the major was made redundant, but before this happened a state-owned company assembled the steel structure. This couldn't have been done quietly – it would be impossible to sneak in many tonnes of steel unnoticed. All this was prepared by a state-owned enterprise.

How were the priests and parishioners involved in the construction?
The success of the construction work depended on the architect. I was responsible for establishing the team: bricklayers, armourers, carpenters, and later, other professional,s to work on fitting and finishing the church. Most priests assigned by the bishop were generally young people with no idea about construction work. I had to educate them so they could understand my intentions. The success of the project also depended on the workers' credentials. Two or three times a week I went to the site and quickly verified the results and cut the amateurs. The crews changed many times. There was no other way – selection is key.

Can you tell us about the design and construction process?
You have no idea how long it all took. The blueprint was the first element – plans, sections and elevations. Later, a ton of other interior design and detail drawings were prepared in 1:10 and 1:1 scale. Every element. One tabernacle has ten drawings. That's millions of work hours. Some drawings are duplicated, because my ideas changed. Sometimes I would design an element and as I was getting ready to go and prepare copies for the construction site, I'd come to the conclusion, while rolling them up, that the solution just wasn't good enough. And off I went, back to the drawing board. I never implemented an idea if I wasn't absolutely sure that it really was a very good idea. That's where the horrendous amount of work came from. I would throw things out and start over again.

On a few occasions I designed in extreme conditions. When I was fifty years old, I had a dreadful fever and while in hospital for two and a half weeks, I designed the parish house for my first church in Kraków, the Church of St. Anthony of Padua.

I was able to design one church and build six others simultaneously. I was the construction manager for each of these churches, present at the site at least once a week. On Tuesdays, I drove a total of 400 km, visiting building sites in Dębica and Krościenko. On Thursdays, I drove to Częstochowa, covering 280 km. Over all the years of designing and building churches, I drove 1.5 million kilometres using fourteen different cars. During the period of fuel rationing, I used eleven times more petrol per month than I was allocated. ■

Antoni Mazur (b. 1922) — Architect, and as of 2016 a 'gold book' graduate from Kraków University of Technology, Mazur has been involved in architecture and religious art since 1952. He is the architect of sixteen completed churches and has designed decorative elements and interior furnishings for fifty other religious buildings, as well as industrial and general construction objects. He has also worked on issues related to monument conservation.

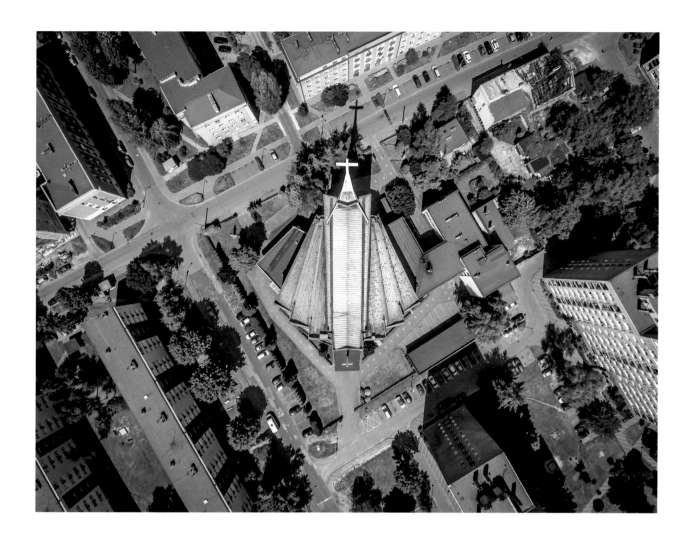

Church of Our Lady of Victory, Częstochowa

architect: Antoni Mazur
construction dates: 1975-2000
GPS: 50.8031, 19.1083

Church of Divine Mercy, Dębica

architect: Antoni Mazur
construction dates: 1982-2001
GPS: 50.049, 21.4266

Solidarity

Interview with Wojciech Jarząbek

Wrocław, 16 September 2015

Solidarity launched mass strikes in Poland during the 1980 Moscow Olympics. It was a movement full of contradictions. Shipyard workers and miners, supported by the intelligentsia and the Church, laid out a series of reforms for the nominal workers' state. Although the liberalization brought on by Solidarity lasted only one-and-a-half years, this period managed to create its own architecture.

Over a short period the government – too weak to indefinitely block the construction of new churches – issued several-thousand building permits. The building of churches got underway on hundreds of prefabricated housing estates. Often lasting more than a decade, they accompanied the entire period of political transformation from Solidarity to the Polish Round Table Talks held in Warsaw in 1989 and the country's accession to the European Union in 2004.

Kuba Snopek: When did construction begin on the Church of Our Lady, Queen of Peace in Wrocław's Popowice housing estate?
Wojciech Jarząbek: The project emerged during the times of Solidarity. I mean both the name of the social movement and the state of interpersonal relations, which is something that had never before and has never again occurred in Polish history. The competition was announced at the end of 1980 and closed in February 1981 and the project was approved and a building permit obtained even before martial law was declared [in December 1981]. The foundation stone was laid in May 1982. At that time I was also a Solidarity activist, among other things I represented a thousand members in the regional assembly. I proudly wore its famous pin. At the construction site people would say: 'Our people have designed it, our people are building it.'

Society was filled with enthusiasm. From 1980 to 1981, there was so much friendliness, kindness. If someone could help out, they did. The construction of new churches enjoyed broad public support. Everyone helped, even the authorities. It was no problem to have a designated plot of land extended so that some parts of the church could be improved. At that time, such projects were being carried out all over Poland, and building and location permits for new places of worship were issued. During martial law, the state no longer fought against the Church and people acted on the building permissions they had previously been granted, and uncompleted projects were taken up again. The Solidarity years created an upsurge that would bear fruit over the following decade.

In mid-1981, a colleague came back from a contract in Kuwait for a couple of days. When he learned about my involvement in trade union activities, he asked: 'What are you doing there?' To which I replied: 'Once we have won our freedom, we will be able to create architecture freely.' Earlier, our strategy had been to talk of design, rather than architecture. Concealment was our regular practice. We never referred to aesthetic criteria, just the functional principles and technical and economic indicators – artistic values had to be smuggled in.

Please tell me more about the plans for the church.
We wanted the body of the church to stand in contrast to, in juxtaposition to, the surrounding architecture, which was built in keeping with the rigours of industrial technology. The church was intended to take the shape of a pyramid. We wanted to have as much space as possible between the blocks of flats and the building, and to avoid the walls opposite forming a tunnel. In the project, we included a bell tower resembling hands folded in prayer. Since the church was dedicated to Our Lady, Queen of Peace, we wanted the roof to be associated with Virgin Mary's robe, something beneath which the worshippers could seek shelter from the PRL's bleak reality.

We also decided to take a stand against all the religious buildings that rely on the cross to determine their function. We assumed that we must design a church whose shape in itself would betray its sacred function. This is why we decided against having a crucifix on the façade. After all, cathedrals don't have them. The building was supposed to reflect the thousand-year history of the Church in Poland in a nonliteral manner. We wanted to include a Romanesque-style portal, but it was later redesigned to accommodate the choir. The building was meant to evoke associations with Gothic architecture, and the skylights paraphrased the buttresses in churches from that period. The interior was supposed to be Baroque in character; the bell tower was modern, and even a bit 'cosmic'. And all this without citing any historical details.

The shape of the building resembles the structure of crystal. Initially, we assumed that it would be clad in polished granite, shiny like a diamond. This idea collapsed after our first talks with the investor, and so we started to look for a more down-to-earth solution. We chose brick, as this is a characteristic material of Wroclaw's religious buildings. We decided that welded steel frames would lend it a strong, sculptural character. I still think that permanently joined steel structures look

Church of Our Lady Queen of Peace, Wrocław

architects: Wacław Hryniewicz, Wojciech Jarząbek, Jan Matkowski
construction dates: 1982-1994
GPS: 51.126, 16.9889

better, more solid than structures with bolted aluminium elements. To me, the latter appear impermanent and cheap.

You will find that we have been greatly inspired by Japanese geometric architecture. As far as postmodernism as such is concerned, when we were creating this project we had no idea about the classifying tendencies of architectural trends at the time.

How did the construction process unfold?

From the outset, we assumed that the building would take a long time to complete. And indeed, the construction took eighteen years. At the end of the 1970s, traditional construction skills were almost extinct – it was assumed that going forward houses would be built from prefabricated elements, so very few new bricklayers or carpenters were being trained and we had few skilled labourers. A few of these labourers were parishioners and they passed on some training to the pensioners and young amateurs who worked on the construction of the church. In a sense, these older workers had been damaged from their years of working in the PRL. They were skilled, but we had to struggle with them a fair bit – not because of the quality of their carpentry or masonry work, but because of the architecture itself and, most importantly, to get them to respect our authority.

I would go up on the scaffolding and explain how to read our drawings. The workers knew their craft very well, but the drawings were often too complicated for them. For three and a half years, I went to the construction site almost every day. We had to keep an eye on the workers all the time. The entrance portal is a bit too high, because the bricklayers got ahead of themselves – instead of demolishing it we redesigned it to avoid annoying the parishioners.

We were also a little bit confused. There was a shortage of literature on traditional construction from the period of the Middle Ages we were interested in. We found some old publications, even some books published before WWII, but they, in turn, contained no information on more advanced technologies. When you create atypical forms, you cannot count on finding ready-made answers in existing textbooks. Coming up with such details requires technical creativity, but the way these details appear should also improve the aesthetic value of the object.

How did the process of building a church differ from that of building other kinds of building in the 1980s?

On other building projects, an architect's influence was far more limited. And in almost all cases the church projects were better paid. I could afford to visit the construction site every day. Later, during martial law, from the moment it became possible to run a private business, I resigned from my job and opened my own practice. At the time, you could get a licence for private undertakings, but you were not allowed to employ anyone. However, being in this position, I didn't have to worry about nipping out of work to go to the site; it was much easier. When it comes to building materials and technological possibilities, it is difficult to imagine today what the working conditions were like at that time. By sheer miracle – and thanks to the great enthusiasm behind the construction of this church – the state-run factory produced not only the standard brick for the façade but custom-made fittings as well and no one contested it.

Do you think that the church in Popowice could be placed under heritage protection?
I think the church is bound to gain listed status. It is ageing beautifully and will last for centuries. It is inimitable, striking and very unusual. I haven't yet seen another church that would be similar to ours. Take its main feature: two towers crowned with a single roof. During one of the anniversary celebrations, Cardinal Henryk Gulbinowicz gave a beautiful sermon, saying, 'We have numerous heritage sites, old and new. Today we are meeting in a brand new historical monument.' ■

Wojciech Jarząbek (b. 1950) — Architect, Jarząbek graduated from Wrocław University of Technology. He founded A+R Studio Wojciech Jarząbek and Partners, where he currently works. In the 1980s, he worked in Kuwait and is considered one of the leading representatives of postmodernism in Poland. He designed the Church of the Blessed Virgin Mary, Queen of Peace, Wrocław.

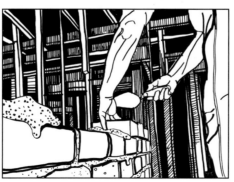

Majesty

Interview with Maciej Hawrylak

Wrocław, 21 April 2016

Although the Catholic Church was in constant conflict with state socialism, the latter was paradoxically also an ally in the creation of sacred architecture. Those who opposed the regime rallied around the Church and were inspired to support the construction of new places of worship. At the same time, the lack of a market economy meant that community-based construction was somewhat easier.

Following the fall of state socialism, a series of monumental churches emerged. However, they weren't built to satisfy the needs of worshippers, but rather the triumphalism of the Polish Catholic Church. Despite the huge scale of the new developments in Warsaw, Toruń, Kraków, and above all Licheń, after 1989 the Church was never again able to construct objects as culturally valuable as those erected in the previous decade.

Kuba Snopek: You were one of the authors of the plan for the Millennium Church in Wrocław.
Maciej Hawrylak: The church was meant to be a monument. The entire idea was extremely pompous: it was meant to mark the beginning of the new millennium and to commemorate the previous one, i.e. the achievements of the post-war period. Plans were drawn up for a Church of the Millennium that would emphasize the 'Polishness' of the region [of Western Poland].

In my opinion, our project won because it took the surrounding urban environment into account. In a way, it proposed a kind of separate world: an entire parish complex, with catechetical quarters, detached from the surrounding buildings and acting as a kind of screen that blocked out the neighbouring housing estate. A semi-circular internal colonnade was planned to separate the church from the annoying street traffic.

At the time, none of the new churches appearing throughout Poland proved that long-standing traditions could be expressed in a contemporary form. We came to the conclusion that it made more sense to design a contemporary copy. Building a replica of Wrocław's gothic cathedral – in a positive sense of the word, not a simple copy-paste job – was intended to refer to traditional roots and to their transformation over time. Moreover, it seemed that turning towards a sensible, adaptable example would be easier to stomach for future users of the building – clergy and parishioners alike.

Was the small church also included in the original design?
Originally it was going to be temporary. It was going to be a miniature of the cathedral with two towers, a chapel – it was going to be a small church for the time of construction only, to be used for consecrations and funerals. The idea was that if the authorities were to block the construction of the main church, then at least something would be left there for the parishioners. However, we know that in projects from the previous era such chapels were often turned into larger churches.

This church was built for the Curia, then, rather than the parish?
The matter was more complicated than usual, because the competition was organized in 1989, before the fall of communism. When the conditions concerning the plot were agreed with the city, no one dreamed that soon everything would be turned upside down. As a result of the changes, a part of the plot facing the water was handed over to a private owner. This created some problems for us – the church didn't buy the land back, and we had to change the location of the planned construction.

The most important part of the process of building the church was ensuring that its symbolic aspect as the Millennium Church is represented. Questions of location, of who it was being built for, were less important. The Curia announced the competition. Later on, the decision was made that it would be a parish church. From that moment onwards, the construction work was led by the parish priest. However, the parish had a hard time establishing itself at that location. A majority of the local residents worked in the army and other uniformed services and resisted the building plans for quite a long time. They were against the creation of this church. Not all of them opposed it, but quite a few did.

The building exceeded both the parish's needs and its financial capacities. We had to employ DIY methods – additional buildings were dropped, as was the intended monumentality; the dimensions of the church were reduced and building materials were changed: whereas the original project included white stone, we ended up using brick and ceramic cladding. Originally, the contemporary stained-glass windows were to be created by a well-known local artist. Unfortunately, the project didn't find favour from the clergy or parishioners. We lost all control over the church furnishings, the connection between the world outside and the ambiance inside. The new parish priest appointed during the construction process carried out the finishings and flooring works himself. The shift in the church's location and omitting of the surrounding complex were natural departures from the original design. There was no need for the catechetical quarters, because religious

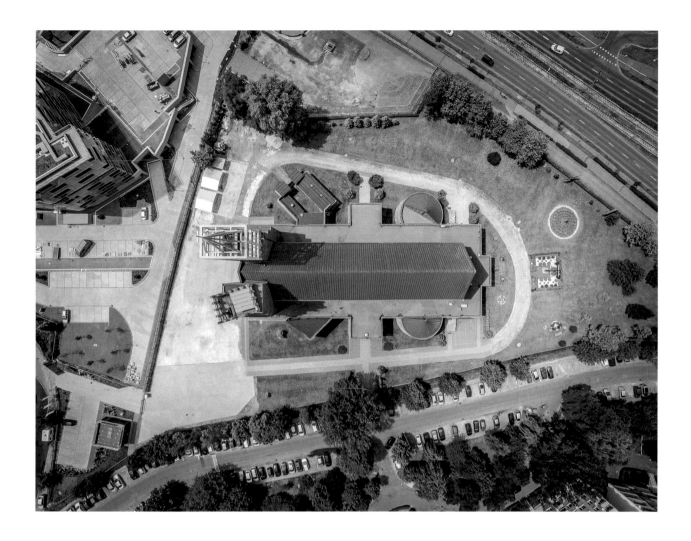

Church of the Redeemer, Wrocław

architects: Jadwiga Grabowska-Hawrylak, Maciej Hawrylak, Wojciech Brzezowski, Ewa Kubica-Hawrylak
construction dates: unknown-1990
GPS: 51.134, 17.0297

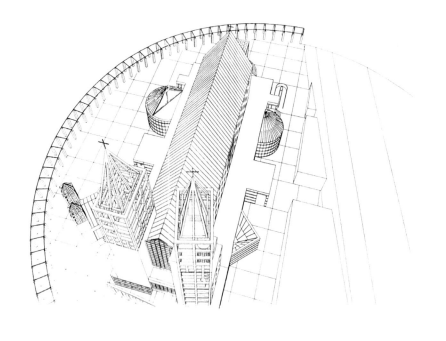

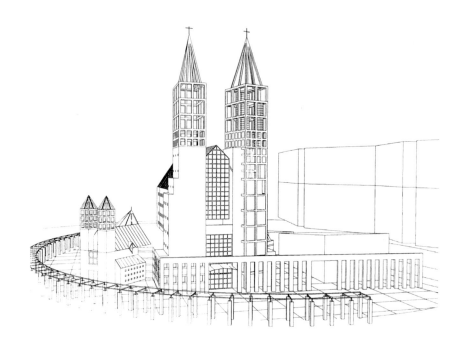

112

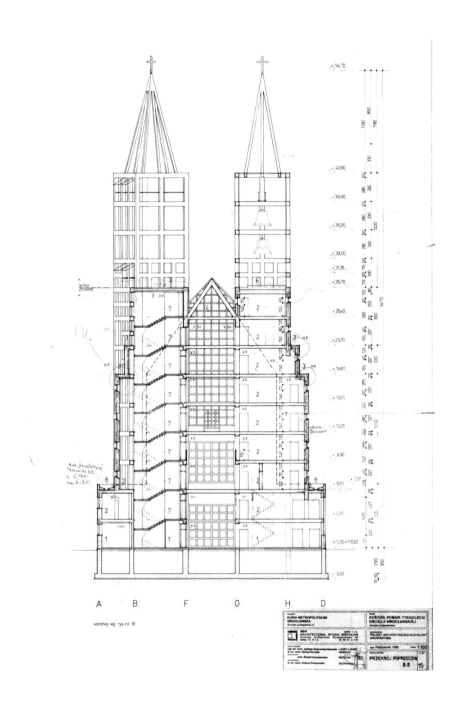

Original designs of the Church of the Redeemer, courtesy of Maciej Hawrylak

education had simply moved into schools. We planned for a field altar at the back of the church, but that was also left out of the result. There were changes to the landscape design as well, which was also restricted for financial reasons. Various elements were reduced, eliminated, never built, left unfinished – the 'complex' gradually disappeared.

Can you tell us about the building process?

We didn't have any schedule, only a deadline when applying for the building permit. Nor was a budget included in the competition's terms and conditions. When the budget was revealed, it turned out that the white travertine stone cladding would be absolutely unfeasible. We faced the dilemma of whether the building might be plastered white. Facing this, the priest suggested that he could purchase bricks of lower-quality instead and asked whether we could swallow it. And so we changed various of the details in a bid to adapt to the shifting reality. Later, this pressure led us to self-censor and simplify our own work. If a problem arose, we'd go to the construction site to try and solve it. We agreed to substitute brick for the stone cladding, to use a variety of construction methods including DIY as well as to have highlanders from Podhale participate in the project – they built everything.

Why the highlanders? First of all, they are very religious. They are famously reliable, accurate, obedient and disciplined. And because they are religious, they listen to the priest, so it is easy to manage them. Priests have confidence in them.

At some point, the construction site descended into chaos. The Curia lost all interest in providing investment and hoped it would be taken care of by the parish. But the parish expected the money to come from the Curia. As a result, the project changes that we submitted to the Curia were never delivered to the planning office and the completed church had no grounds on which to receive a civil use approval. We tried to make up for this later, but the matter turned out to be rather confounding. The completed part of the project could no longer be replaced with a different project. At the time, this would have been seen as a land-use violation that required legalizing the status quo, which, in turn, would require that a new project be submitted. Everyone we asked about how to get out of this catch-22 situation told us: 'Once we have the documentation, the updated project, we can talk. If there is no documentation, there is nothing to talk about.' Again, this was precisely the problem: the architects, builders and others would have to produce this new documentation. Things were not like they are today, when you have digitized projects able to be printed as many times as you like. On top of that, we lost some of our documentation in the 1997 flood. Today we would need to create an inventory and a new design project. At this point, a lot of money is still needed to complete the project. The church is still under construction and increasingly more and more elements will differ from the original design.

Oh well! In the past, some churches took as long as three hundred years to complete and somehow it didn't bother anyone [laughter].

What advice would you give to an architect setting out to design a church?
I did not design a church but a millennial monument, which is something entirely different. It was intended to be pompous. I don't even know if I've gained any experience in church design. Also, I didn't get a chance to build it from start to finish. Along the way, the setting and conditions changed. The church-monument turned into a parish church. We had neither time nor the opportunity to change its proportions, shape, location or the interior's orientation. Nor did we examine the neighbourhood again.

A church is something entirely different. It's about social development, culture, roots and our ancestors. In our churches, I would rather see humility, restraint, attentiveness and silence – all the elements that allow us to be among others and at the same time keep connected with the majesty of God. But is such the culture of Catholic churches? Not necessarily. ■

Dr Maciej Hawrylak (b. 1952) — Architect, Hawrylak teaches at his alma mater, Wrocław University of Technology. He is the Vice President of the Wrocław branch of Stowarzyszenie Architektów Polskich [Association of Polish Architects, SARP] and runs his own design office. He has won numerous competitions and, together with his mother, Jadwiga Grabowska-Hawrylak, designed the Church-Monument of the Millennium in Wrocław.

Church of Our Lady of Licheń, Licheń Stary

architect: Barbara Bielecka
construction dates: 1994-2004
GPS: 52.3236, 18.3582

Church of the Holy Cross and Our Lady Healer of the Sick, Katowice

architects: Henryk Buszko, Aleksander Franta
construction dates: 1979-1993
GPS: 50.2757, 18.9718

Church of the Holy Cross and Our Lady Healer of the Sick, Katowice

architects: Henryk Buszko, Aleksander Franta
construction dates: 1979-1993
GPS: 50.2757, 18.9718

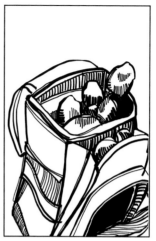

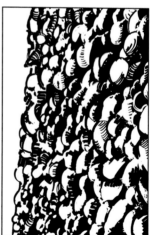

Church of Our Lady Queen of Poland, Kraków

architect: Wojciech Pietrzyk
construction dates: 1967-1977
GPS: 50.085, 20.0291

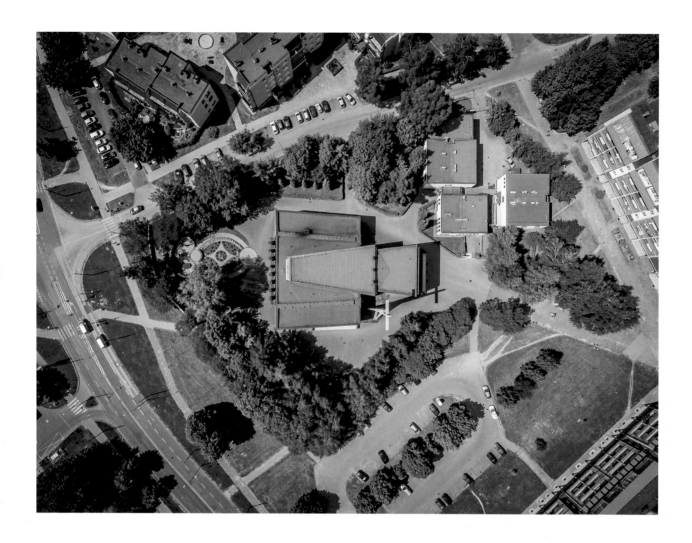

Church of St John the Baptist, Tychy

architects: Zbigniew Weber, Tadeusz Szczęsny
construction dates: 1957-1958
GPS: 50.1163, 18.9794

Church of St Joseph the Worker, Kraśnik

architect: Aleksander Holas
construction dates: 1978-1998
GPS: 50.9596, 22.1555

Church of Our Lady of Victory, Bydgoszcz

architect: Aleksander Holas
construction dates: 1980-1990
GPS: 53.1308, 18.0468

Church of Blessed Virgin Mary the Helper, Piła

architect: Aleksander Holas
construction dates: 1978-2000
GPS: 53.1504, 16.7133

Church of St Brother Albert Chmielowski, Częstochowa

architect: Aleksander Holas
construction dates: 1981-2001
GPS: 50.8506, 19.1164

Church of St Barbara the Virgin and Martyr, Rudniki

architect: Aleksander Holas
construction dates: 1988-1992
GPS: 50.5213, 19.4214

Church of St Maxmilian Maria Kolbe, Konin

architect: Aleksander Holas
construction dates: 1973-1981
GPS: 52.2304, 18.2439

Church of Divine Mercy, Bielsk Podlaski

architect: Andrzej Chwalibóg
construction dates: 1992-2001
GPS: 52.7543, 23.173

Church of St Maximilian Kolbe, Kolnica

architect: Andrzej Chwalibóg
construction dates: unknown-1986
GPS: 53.7867, 23.0498

Church of Our Lady of Częstochowa, Kosmolów

architect: unknown
construction dates: 1975-1984
GPS: 50.2712, 19.6646

Church of Our Lady of Mercy, Suwałki

architect: unknown
construction dates: 1982-2000
GPS: 54.124, 22.9484

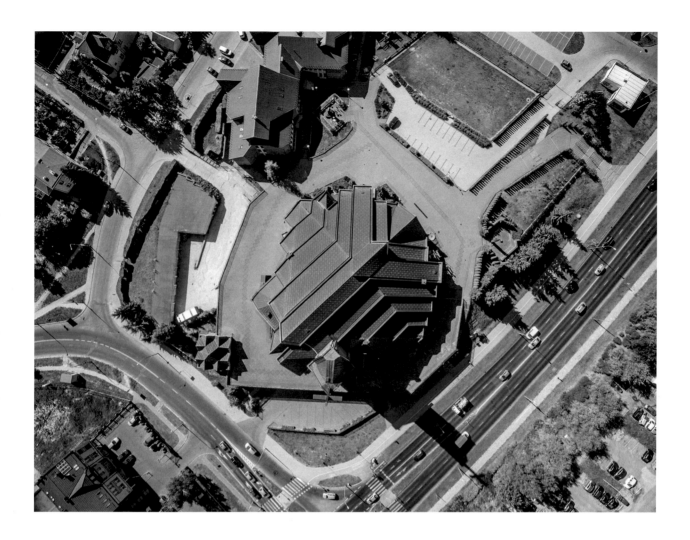

Church of Christ the Saviour, Olsztyn

architect: JASTRZĘBSKI Design Studio
construction dates: unknown
GPS: 53.7652, 20.5041

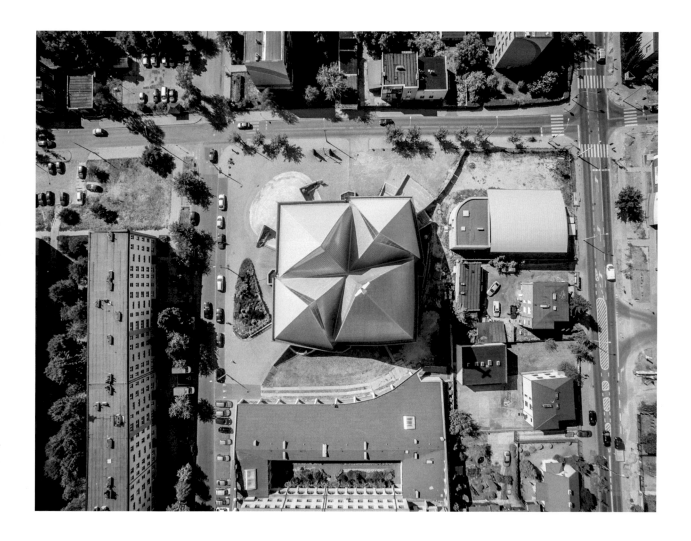

Church of Our Lady Queen of the World, Radom

architect: Wojciech Gęsiak
construction dates: 1982-2012
GPS: 51.4047, 21.1729

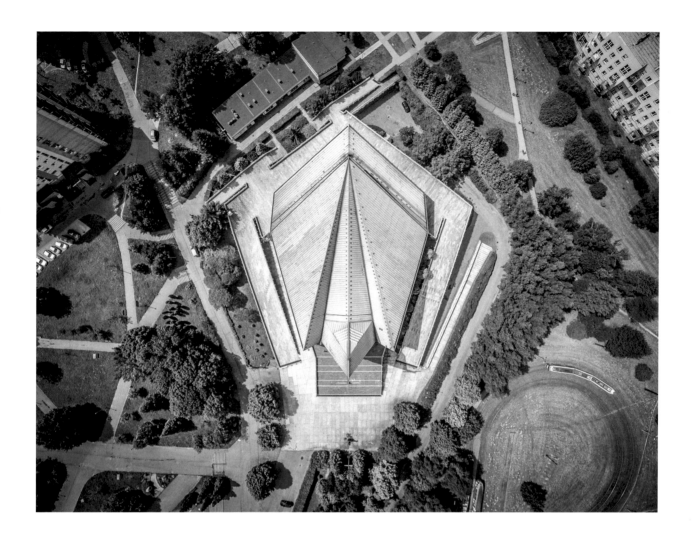

Church of St Maximilian Kolbe, Kraków

architect: Józef Dutkiewicz
construction dates: 1976-1983
GPS: 50.0945, 19.9966

Church of Our Lady of Częstochowa, Lubcza

architects: Zbigniew Ciok, Bogdan Grządziela
construction dates: 1989-1994
GPS: 50.4772, 20.3379

Church of the Holy Apostles Peter and Paul, Siedliska

architect: unknown
construction dates: unknown-1987
GPS: 49.7273, 20.9861

Church of the Transfiguration of Jesus Christ, Częstochowa

architect: unknown
construction dates: 1981-1990
GPS: 50.7929, 19.0179

Church of Our Lady Queen of Polish Martyrs, Warsaw

architect: Jerzy Kumelowski
construction dates: 1994-2000
GPS: 52.2396, 21.0809

Church of St Eugene de Mazenod, Kędzierzyn-Koźle

architect: Alfons Kupka
construction dates: 1976-1998
GPS: 50.341, 18.1995

Church of Our Lady of Częstochowa, Kraków

architects: Krzysztof Dyga, Andrzej Nasfeter
construction dates: 1984-1994
GPS: 50.0756, 20.0455

Church of St Stanislaus Kostka, Wrocław

architects: Stefan Müller, Barbara Jaworska
construction dates: 1984-2006
GPS: 51.0893, 17.0431

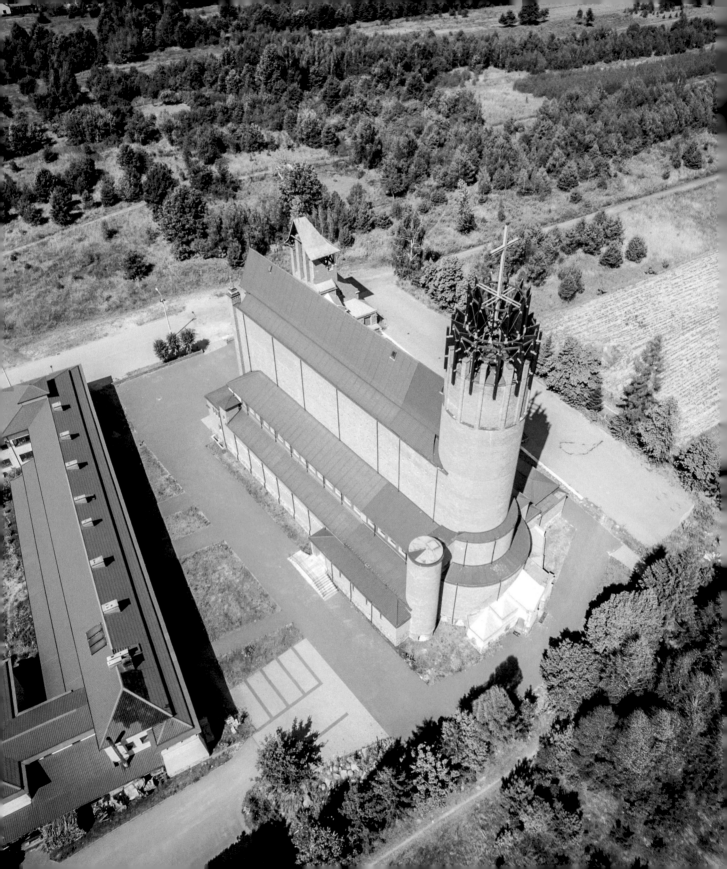

Church of the Holy Virgin Mary the Queen of Poland, Pionki

architects: O. Jagiełło, J. Szczepaniak-Dzikowski, J. Laskowski
construction dates: 1985-2009
GPS: 51.4806, 21.4512

Church of St Anne, Myszków

architect: Wiktor Baran
construction dates: 1986-1992
GPS: 50.5482, 19.3006

Church of our Lady of Fatima, Kraków

architects: Przemysław Gawor, Małgorzata Grabacka, Jan Grabacki
construction dates: 1983-1998
GPS: 50.041, 19.9308

Church of St Anthony of Padua, Zduńska Wola

architect: Szczepan Baum
construction dates: 1976-1987
GPS: 51.592, 18.9515

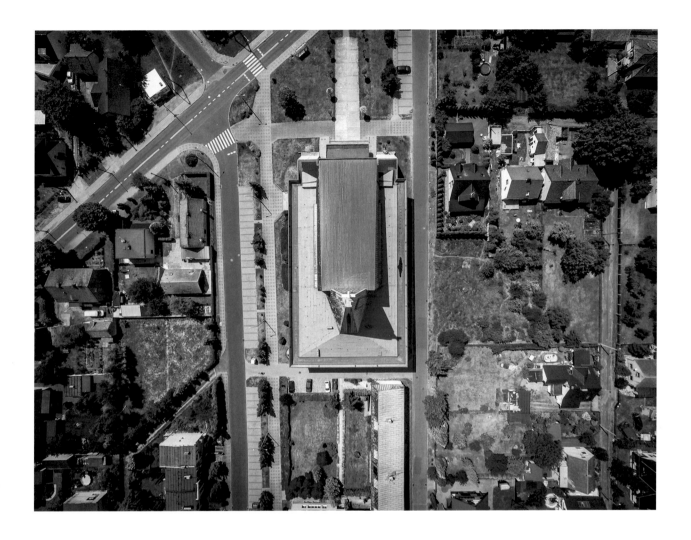

Church of St Hyacinth, Opole

architect: Jakub Schröter
construction dates: 1977-1989
GPS: 50.6691, 17.9795

Church of the Holy Virgin Mary the Queen of Poland, Zawiercie

architect: unknown
construction dates: 1974-unknown
GPS: 50.4789, 19.4406

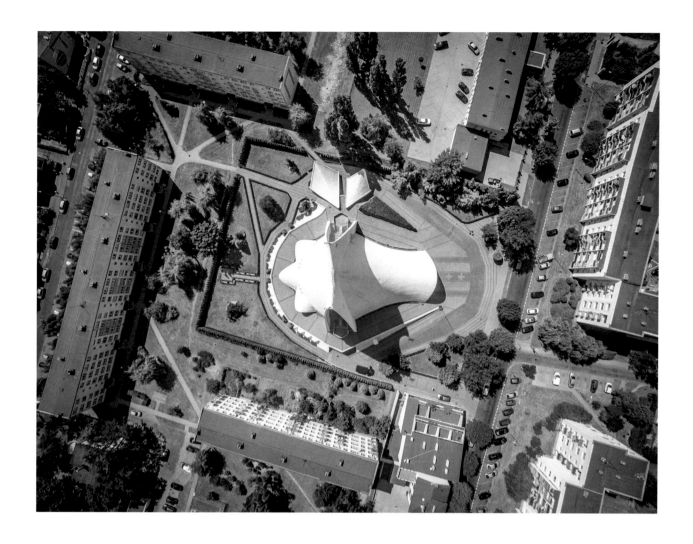

Church of Divine Mercy, Kalisz

architects: Jerzy Kuźmienko, Andrzej Fajans
construction dates: 1977-1989
GPS: 51.7491, 18.0781

Church of the Immacculate Virgin Mary, Nowy Sącz

architect: Leszek Filar
construction dates: 1982-1992
GPS: 49.6161, 20.7158

Church of St Maximilian Kolbe, Kicznia

architect: Eugeniusz Baziak
construction dates: 1983-1989
GPS: 49.5913, 20.4305

Church of Divine Mercy, Kielce

architect: Marian Sztafrowski
construction dates: 1981-2000
GPS: 50.8787, 20.6042

Church of the Holy Virgin Mary the Queen of Poland, Gromnik

architect: Zbigniew Zjawin
construction dates: 1983-1991
GPS: 49.8396, 20.9556

Church of Christ the Saviour, Gdańsk

architect: Szczepan Baum
construction dates: 1983-1992
GPS: 54.4248, 18.4641

Church of St Joseph the Worker, Kielce

architects: Władzsław Pieńkowski, Marian Szymanowski, Kinga Pieńkowska-Osińska
construction dates: 1975-1995
GPS: 50.8893, 20.6418

Church of Pope St Pius V, Dęblin

architect: Marian Skowroński
construction dates: 1975-1981
GPS: 51.562, 21.8572

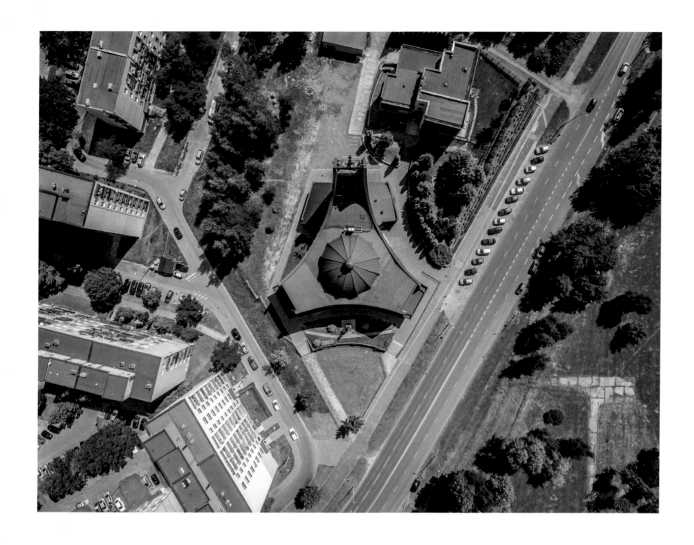

Church of St Maxmilian Maria Kolbe, Dąbrowa Górnicza

architect: Zygmunt Fagas
construction dates: 1986-2003
GPS: 50.3167, 19.1726

Church of St Jadwiga Queen of Poland, Lublin

architect: Roman Orlewski
construction dates: 1982-1985
GPS: 51.2681, 22.5439

Church of Our Lady Queen of Poland, Toruń

architect: Czesław Sobociński
construction dates: 1986-1993
GPS: 53.0285, 18.6523

Church of St Joseph the Worker, Ustrzyki Dolne

architects: Leonard Reppel, Wacław Mazur
construction dates: 1981-1991
GPS: 49.4354, 22.5818

Church of the Blessed Virgin Mary Mother of the Church, Orły

architect: Leonard Reppel
construction dates: 1981-1986
GPS: 49.8718, 22.8106

Church of the Holy Spirit, Mielec

architects: Stanisław Kokoszka, Kazimierz Flag
construction dates: 1983-1987
GPS: 50.295, 21.4203

Church of Our Lady the Queen of Poland, Elbląg

architect: Zygmunt Twardowski
construction dates: 1977-2013
GPS: 54.1702, 19.4012

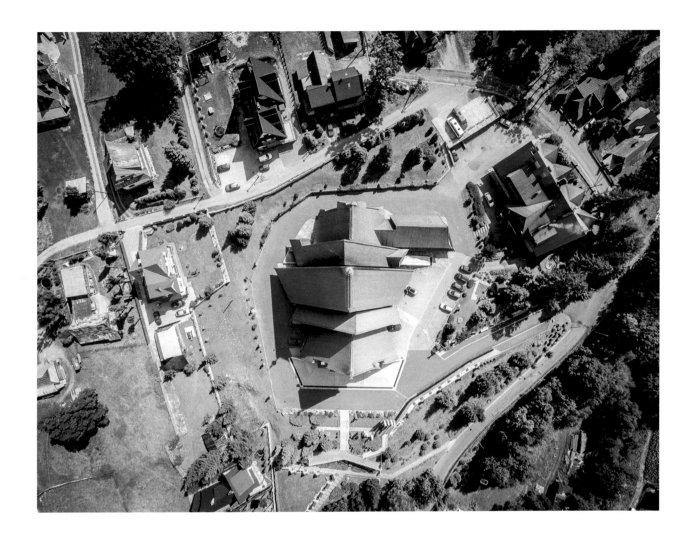

Church of Our Lady Revealing the Miraculous Medal, Zakopane

architect: Tadeusz Gawłowski
construction dates: 1981-1988
GPS: 49.307, 19.9968

Church of St Joseph, Spouse of the Blessed Virgin Mary, Lublin

architect: Stanisław Fijałkowski
construction dates: 1982-1995
GPS: 51.2402, 22.5299

Church of Mary, Star of the New Evangelization and St John Paul II, Toruń

architect: Andrzej Ryczek
construction dates: 2012-2015
GPS: 53.018, 18.5185

Church of the Blessed Virgin Mary Mother of the Church, Świdnik

architects: Leopold Taraszkiewicz, Andrzej Różeński
construction dates: 1977-1985
GPS: 51.2123, 22.6979

Church of St John Cantius, Kraków

architect: Krzysztof Bień
construction dates: 1983-1992
GPS: 50.0799, 19.8892

Church of the Holy Family, Poznań

architects: Włodzimierz Wojciechowski, Bogdan Celichowski, Wojciech Kasprzycki
construction dates: 1983-1992
GPS: 52.3866, 16.8667

Church of Our Lady of the Rosary, Gdańsk

architects: Leopold Taraszkiewicz, M. Chomicki
construction dates: 1972-1976
GPS: 54.4071, 18.5845

The Temple of Divine Providence, Warsaw

architect: Wojciech Szymborski
construction dates: 2002-2016
GPS: 52.1586, 21.0722

Church of St Casimir, Białystok

architect: Jan Krutula
construction dates: 1983-1993
GPS: 53.1497, 23.1225

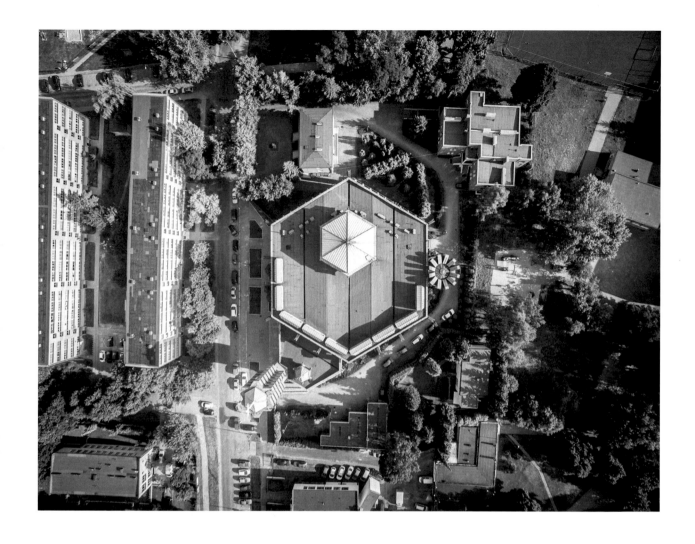

Church of Our Lady of Sorrows, Łódź

architects: Leszek Łukoś, Ludwik Mackiewicz
construction dates: 1973-1976
GPS: 51.7954, 19.3887

Church of Nativity, Poznań

architects: Jerzy Liśniewicz, Jan Sosnowski
construction dates: 1995-2007
GPS: 52.4594, 16.9203

Church of the Visitation of Virgin Mary, Będzin

architect: Ryszard Kumor
construction dates: 1981-2000
GPS: 50.3195, 19.1163

Church of the Divine Mercy, Kwidzyn

architect: Unknown
construction dates: 1981-1994
GPS: 53.7294, 18.9375

Church of St Lawrence, Wrocław

architects: Wiktor Dziębaj, Zenon Prętczyński
construction dates: 1978-1980
GPS: 51.1184, 17.0687

Church of St Joseph the Artisan, Przedbórz

architect: Władysław Pieńkowski
construction dates: 1972-1979
GPS: 50.1843, 21.7401

Church of St Anthony of Padua, Krynica-Zdrój

architects: Ewa Węcławowicz-Gyurkovich, Jacek Gyurkovich
construction dates: 1982-1993
GPS: 49.4089, 20.9554

Church of St Jude Thaddeus and Brother St Albert, Mirocin

architect: Władysław Jagiełło
construction dates: 1983-1985
GPS: 51.7776, 15.5453

Church of St Joseph the Worker, Wołyńce

architect: Jan Pełka
construction dates: 1979-1987
GPS: 52.122, 22.2182

Church of St Joseph the Artisan, Tarnowiec

architect: unknown
construction dates: 1983-1990
GPS: 49.9876, 20.9866

Church of Our Lady of the Rosary, Żurawiczki

architect: Leonard Reppel
construction dates: 1981-1985
GPS: 50.0281, 22.5119

Church of Divine Mercy and Blessed Sister Faustyna Kowalska, Toruń

architect: Jerzy Matusiak-Tusiacki
construction dates: 1992-1998
GPS: 53.0318, 18.604

Church of the Visitation of the Blessed Virgin Mary, Poznań

architects: Marek Eibl, Stanisław Sołtyk
construction dates: 1979-1996
GPS: 52.384, 16.9535

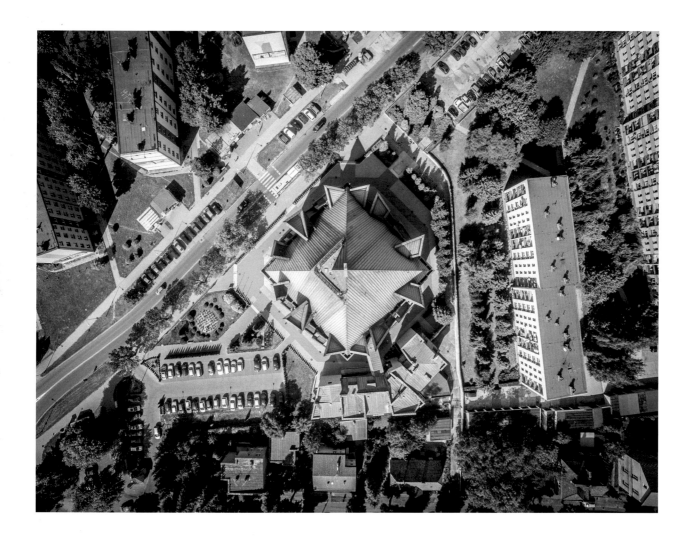

Church of Divine Mercy, Tarnów

architects: Andrzej Boratyński, Piotr Łabowicz, Andrzej Skoczek
construction dates: 1984-1991
GPS: 50.0192, 20.9754

Church of the Last Supper, Lublin

architects: Zbigniew Szeliga, Bożena Szeliga
construction dates: 1987-1989
GPS: 51.2534, 22.5227

Church of the Holy Virgin Mary, Help of Christians, Rumia

architect: Leopold Taraszkiewicz
construction dates: 1977-1998
GPS: 54.5667, 18.3987

Church of the Most Sacred Heart of Jesus, Gdynia

architects: Leopold Taraszkiewicz, M. Chomicki, J. Borowski
construction dates: 1957-1966
GPS: 54.5183, 18.5361

Church of Our Lady of Mercy, Radom

architects: Leopold Taraszkiewicz, Antoni Taraszkiewicz, Andrzej Różeński
construction dates: 1978-1988
GPS: 51.4074, 21.1607

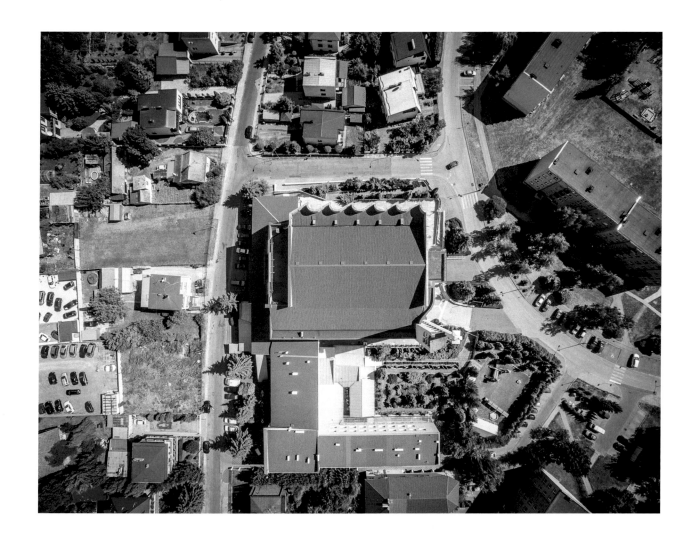

Church of Our Lady of Perpetual Help, Tarnobrzeg

architect: Gerard Pająk
construction dates: 1981-1988
GPS: 50.5791, 21.6845

Church of Divine Providence, Wrocław

architect: Tadeusz Zipser
construction dates: 1989-under construction
GPS: 51.1149, 16.9575

Church of the Holy Spirit, Wrocław

architects: Waldemar Wawrzyniak, Jerzy Wojnarowicz, Wojciech Święcicki, Tadeusz Zipser
construction dates: 1973-1994
GPS: 51.0847, 17.0498

AFTERWORD

Afterword

The research project we have presented here on Day-VII Architecture began in 2013. It comprises a series of modules, including: a database of Roman Catholic churches built in Poland post-1945, compiled from scratch in collaboration with an Internet audience; a crowdsourcing website on which anyone can submit and review data relating to their parish church, and upload photographs and memories; a collection of thousands of photographs from several photographers; a set of comic strip-illustrations explaining the details of our project; a set of maps and infographics based on the data collected; dozens of interviews with church architects; an archive of original blueprints; and an essay describing the genesis and methods of church construction in Poland after 1945.

To date, we have presented our research to the public in the form of a number of exhibitions in locations including Warsaw, Poznań, Wrocław, London, Berlin, Prague, Logroño, and at the 2017 Chicago Architecture Biennial. Various elements of our research have also been presented in the media and at academic conferences. In 2016, we published a Polish-language guidebook containing most of our findings. We are now extremely pleased to be publishing our research in English for the first time.

The aim of the English-language edition is, firstly, to present to foreign readers the vast and diverse phenomenon that we name Day-VII Architecture. For this reason, the English version, done in collaboration with DOM Publishers, is very different to the original Polish edition. Instead of presenting our analyses, we give voice here to the church architects themselves, who talk in detail about the challenges they faced with certain buildings. Instead of publishing architectural plans and blueprints, we have decided to focus on photographs of the completed objects (all photographed from the same perspective and height of one hundred metres). We have summed up the historical part in a brief chronology that presents the wider context and background of the construction work, and replaced the data analysis section with a single map and infographic.

Although there are some studies that focus on individual architects or regions of the country, our project is the first to take a global look at the construction of churches in socialist Poland. Due to the semi-formal nature of this phenomenon, collecting data was a challenge. Numerous churches were built without any official building permits (especially in rural parishes and in south-eastern Poland); and in many cases the documentation submitted to state authorities differs wildly from what was actually built. For this reason, we decided while building the database to crowdsource much of the information rather than to rely on getting it all from official archives. The information we have gathered was thus done with the help of hundreds of people from all over Poland, who have added or amended data on the project's website, http://architektura7dnia.com

Such challenges led us to develop our own original research methodology. Following an analysis of the publicly available database of the Institute for Catholic Church Statistics (Instytut Statystyki Kościoła Katolickiego, ISKK), we compiled a list of approximately 3,700 Catholic parishes in which the new churches were located. We designed and coded our own tools for crowdsourcing and reviewing data, analyzing and comparing photographs, mapping the housing estates, and calculating the surface area of buildings. The data was also used to select the most interesting case studies for further analysis. We conducted local inspections in the churches selected, as well as interviews with priests, construction workers and architects. This material was then complemented by research in local SARP archives and theological seminaries, and by a review of architectural press and literature.

Our hope is that the work carried out thus far will serve as a basis for further research. We are more than happy to share our data with researchers from other fields whose findings can enrich our outlook with different perspectives. We have already made the database available to scholars in the fields of sociology, political science and economics.

We plan to supplement this publication with an academic essay in English to describe our research thus far. We would also like to locate Polish religious architecture in the context of Eastern European postmodernism. Last but not least, the DIY method of communal construction, accidentally 'invented' by church builders and later forgotten in the 1990s, has inspired us to further explore possibilities for crowdsourcing in relation to architecture and development. To be continued...

Authors
Izabela Cichońska,
Karolina Popera,
Kuba Snopek

Project management
Kuba Snopek

Exhibitions
Izabela Cichońska

Archival research and database
Karolina Popera

Production
Bogna Świątkowska,
Bęc Zmiana Foundation

Drone photos
Igor Snopek (pages: 34, 37, 48, 51, 58- 64, 67, 70, 71,
82- 84, 87, 92- 95, 99, 105, 108, 111, 122,123, 126,127,
132-277)

Photos
Maciej Lulko (pages: 6-7, 55, 72, 74, 80, 88, 91, 96, 100,
103, 104, 106, 114-115, 118-119, 120, 121, 124, 125, 128,
130, 131),
Max Avdeev (page 10)

Illustrations
Izabela Cichońska (pages: 38-40, 45, 52, 57, 69, 76-79,
107, 129)

Editing
Kuba Snopek

Translation
Joanna Figiel

Copyediting
Steve Corcoran

Design
Damian Makowski

Transcription of interviews
Rebeka Czaja, Anna Deska, Anna Ek, Piotr Kuchejda,
Janusz Magoński, Hanna Moskal, Katarzyna Pabich,
Zuzanna Robutka, Jakub Szumilas, Joanna Żak

Website
Alexandr Ayoupov,
Kuba Snopek

Data Analysis
Tomasz Świetlik, Alexandr Ayoupov, Szymon Pifczyk

Data Collection
Agnieszka Baryła, Daria Cichoń, Szymon Ciupiński,
Anna Deska, Katarzyna Dudycz, Karolina Dyjach,
Marta Gruca, Emilia Karwowska, Tomasz Koczur,
Magdalena Koźluk, Katarzyna Malinowska, Agata
Matczuk, Wojciech Mazan, Kamila Milewska, Ewa
Mirska, Anna Młodzianowska, Magdalena Owczarek,
Katarzyna Pabich, Anna Piasecka, Łukasz Pieńczykowski,
Karolina Popera, Marcin Semeniuk, Agata Stasiak,
Agnieszka Zawistowska, Julita Zembrowska

**Our collaborators, who worked on the previous
editions of the project:**
Max Avdeev, Anna Cymer, Monika Drab, Urszula
Drabińska, Anna B. Gregorczyk, Jakub Jezierski, Maciej
Lizak, Nicholas W. Moore, dr Krzysztof Nawratek, Ela
Petruk, Piotr Szukiel, Przemysław Witkowski

The experts, who inspired and assisted our research:
Alexey Ametov, Vasiliy Auzan, Maria Drėmaitė,
Maciej Frąckowiak, Lida Gumieniuk, Alicja Gzowska,
Fr Krzysztof Janiak, Aleksandra Kędziorek, Tomasz
Kmita-Skarsgård, Fr Marian Matula, Fr Czesław
Mazur, Izabela Mironowicz, Michał Murawski,
Dr Krzysztof Nawratek, Vladimir Paperny, Piotr
Szukiel, Bogna Świątkowska, Kamila Twardowska

The architects, who agreed to be interviewed for the project:

Jerzy Gurawski, Dr Maciej Hawrylak, Wojciech Jarząbek, Jerzy Kopyciak, Prof Konrad Kucza-Kuczyński, Prof Adam Lisik, Dr Romuald Loegler, Jerzy Matusiak-Tusiacki, Antoni Mazur, Stanisław Niemczyk, Dr Andrzej Poniewierka, Tadeusz Szukała, Dr Antoni Taraszkiewicz, Marian Tunikowski, Prof Waldemar Wawrzyniak, Prof Tadeusz Zipser

For facilitating access to various archives:

SARP Warsaw, SARP Częstochowa, Fr Paweł Kostrzewa, Hubert Wąsek, Wrocław Development Bureau, The Library of the Papal Theological Department, and the library of the Wrocław University of Science and Technology.

Printing

Master Print Super Offset S.R.L., Bucharest
www.masterprint.ro

Partner

Adam Mickiewicz Institute

Co-publisher

Fundacja Bęc Zmiana

bęc zmiana

The publication has been supported by the Adam Mickiewicz Institute as part of POLSKA 100 – the international cultural programme accompanying the centenary of Poland regaining independence.

The Adam Mickiewicz Institute's celebratory international programme of Polish culture includes several hundred cultural events ranging from film productions to exhibitions, concerts and theatre performances.

POLSKA 100 international cultural programme is financed by the Ministry of Culture and National Heritage of the Republic of Poland as part of the multi-annual programme NIEPODLEGŁA 2017–2022.

www.culture.pl

Day-VII Architecture was part of the interdisciplinary project "Church of Beauty and Kitsch" coordinated by Impart 2016 Festival Office – the organizer of the European Capital of Culture Wrocław 2016.
The project was co-financed by the Ministry of Culture and National Heritage of the Republic of Poland.

EUROPEAN CAPITAL
OF CULTURE

WROCŁAW 2016
European Capital of Culture

The *Deutsche Bibliothek* lists this publication in the *Deutsche Nationalbibliografie*; detailed bibliographic data is available on the internet at *http://dnb.d-nb.de*

ISBN 978-3-86922-741-2

© 2019 by DOM publishers, Berlin
www.dom-publishers.com